CHRISTOPHER ISHERWOOD

CHRISTOPHER ISHERWOOD

A Personal Memoir

JOHN LEHMANN

WEIDENFELD AND NICOLSON · LONDON

The publishers would like to thank Rachel Gould, Miles Huddleston, Charles Osborne, Ian Irvine and Alexis Rassine for their help with preparing the manuscript for press.

First published in Great Britain by
George Weidenfeld & Nicolson Ltd
91 Clapham High Street, London SW4 7TA

ISBN 0 297 79179 6

Printed in Great Britain by The Bath Press, Avon

CONTENTS

LIST OF ILLUSTRATIONS   vii

FRONTISPIECE   1

A PERSONAL MEMOIR   5

AFTERWORD   111

INDEX   144

LIST OF ILLUSTRATIONS

Between pages 70 and 71

Isherwood photographed by Howard Coster in 1936 (National Portrait Gallery)

W.H.Auden, Isherwood and Stephen Spender (Hulton Picture Library)

Isherwood and Heinz Neddermayer (John Lehmann)

Snapshot of Isherwood taken by Benjamin Britten (National Portrait Gallery)

Scenes from the original production of *The Dog Beneath the Skin* (Mander & Mitchenson Theatre Collection)

Isherwood and W.H.Auden departing for China (Hulton Picture Library)

Isherwood and W.H.Auden photographed by Louise Dahl-Wolfe in 1938 (Staley Wise Gallery, New York)

John Lehmann in 1939, photographed by Hans Wild (John Lehmann)

Isherwood, E.M.Forster and William Plomer photographed by

William Caskey (King's College, Cambridge)
Isherwood in the early fifties (John Lehmann)
Beatrix, John and Rosamond Lehmann (John Lehmann)
Isherwood photographed by Tony Eyles in 1965 (Daily Herald
Picture Library)
John Lehmann photographed by Christopher Barker in 1980 for
his book, *Portraits of Poets*, Carcanet, 1986 (John Lehmann)
Isherwood and Don Bachardy photographed by Stathis Orphanos
in 1972 (Don Bachardy)
A Lithograph of Isherwood and Don Bachardy by David
Hockney, 1976 (Barry Artist)

Pages ix, 5, 111 and 145

Drawings of Isherwood by Don Bachardy done during
Christopher's last illness in September 1985.

Page 56

The cover of *Penguin New Writing*, No. 7 (John Lehmann)

FRONTISPIECE

W hen I first met him in 1932, Christopher Isherwood was twenty-eight years old, having been born in August 1904 at one of the two rather grand houses that belonged to his family, Wyberslegh Hall, High Lane, Cheshire. His father was a professional soldier, though rather reluctantly as his real interest lay in the arts; music and painting in particular. He was himself a water-colourist with a certain individual gift which he never had time or opportunity to develop. His taste was shared by his wife, Christopher's mother, though the son doesn't seem to have realized it until many years later, when he read his mother's diaries. His father was killed in the Battle of the Somme in 1916, though for a long time he was only acknowledged officially as 'missing'.

At his prep school Christopher found himself a fellow-pupil of Wystan Auden, but he did not become close to him until they were both at university, Auden at Oxford, Christopher at Cambridge. At his public school, Repton, he met Edward Upward, and formed a devoted friendship with him. They were both intensely interested in writing, Christopher in writing novels,

Upward in poetry, though he afterwards turned to fiction. When he began to publish, Christopher, with only one exception, always sought to find approval first from Upward. This was the more remarkable, as Christopher by then had acknowledged himself as homosexual, and Upward was always heterosexual. At Repton, they created a fantasy world together, which developed at Cambridge into Mortmere, which occupied much of their imaginations for many years, becoming more and more extravagant as time went on. They used to write stories of Mortmere to one another every night, many of which have survived, but are not publishable, the only exception being 'The Railway Accident', which was eventually published in America. Christopher scrapped his first novel, keeping only the title, 'Lions and Shadows', for future use. He also scrapped the second novel, 'Christopher Garland', but the third novel, 'Seascape with Figures' turned into *All the Conspirators* and was accepted and published by Cape in May 1928. In spite of having won an outstanding scholarship to Corpus Christi, Christopher gradually disengaged himself from Cambridge, making a joke of his exams, to the scandal of his tutor and his family. While he was at Cambridge he was inveigled into the film world by his friend Roger Burford, and it remained a passion for him to the end of his life. At the beginning of his adult life he only had two small allowances to live off, one from his Uncle Henry (whose heir he was) and one from his mother. He determined to make his living by writing.

This book has been compiled almost exclusively from Christopher's letters to me, and diary extracts by me made at the same time. Nearly all my letters to Christopher up to and including the duration of the war have disappeared. For the extracts I use I have relied on the typewritten copies which I kept myself. There are a few letters to Christopher after the war: these were found by Don Bachardy in their house after Christopher's death, and were sent to me then. I include some of them towards the end of this book. Even so I must say that the later letters have many gaps in them, and therefore the information in them is lost for good.

I have had the great advantage of being able to use photographs of some of the drawings made by Don Bachardy from the life in Christopher's last months. My special thanks go to Don Bachardy for the permission to use them.

A PERSONAL MEMOIR

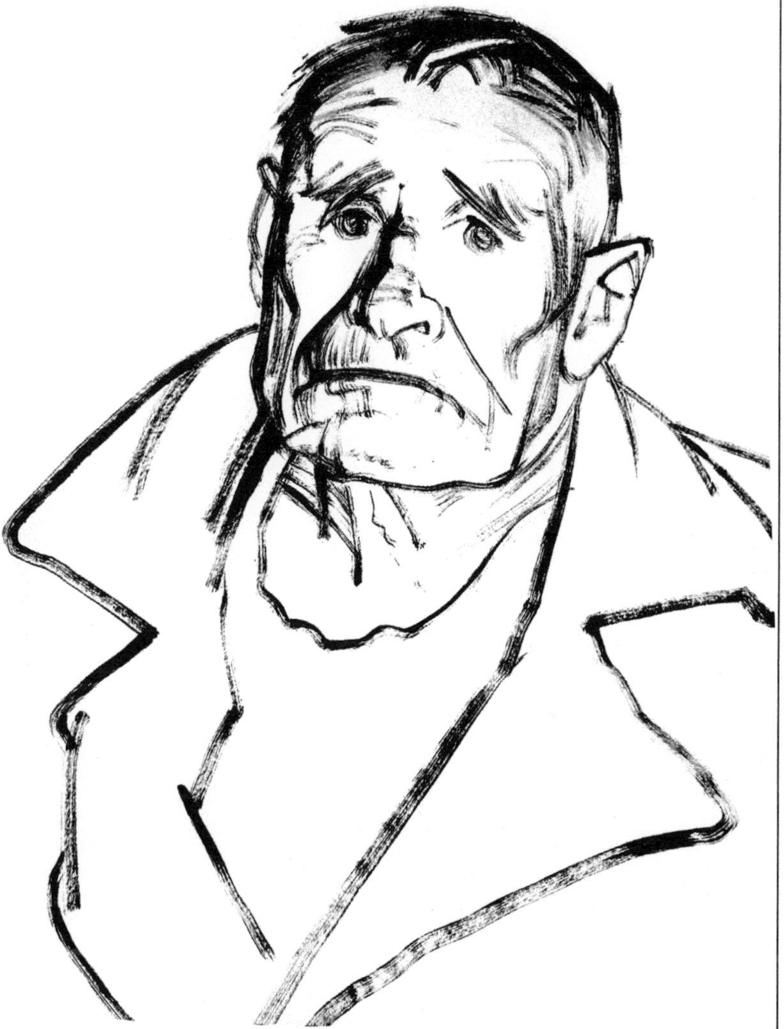

I

n the early days of January 1931 I found myself as trainee manager in Leonard and Virginia Woolf's Hogarth Press, rather to my surprise. I say 'to my surprise' because it all happened so fast. My parents had encouraged me, while I was at Cambridge, to set my sights for the future on the Foreign Office, in which members of our family had already had distinguished careers. I set myself to study French and German intensively, but when I came down from Cambridge a new idea turned up. My godmother Violet Hammersley had friends in the Prints and Drawings Department of the British Museum, and thought she could get me in. I had already started on a tour to acquaint myself with the main Continental museums where I could study their collections of drawings and water-colours, when something happened to alter the whole perspective of the future for me. My Cambridge friend Julian Bell, nephew of Virginia Woolf, had his first book of.poems accepted by the Hogarth Press, and told Leonard and Virginia that he had a friend who also wrote poetry, which both he and George (Dadie) Rylands thought very promising. He also told them that I was interested in printing.

At that moment the Woolfs were looking – not for the first time – for some young man they could train to manage the Press for them and eventually become their partner.

The result was that I prepared a first book of poems to submit to them, which was accepted more quickly than I expected. In his letter of acceptance Leonard cautiously hinted that they would be interested to sound me about joining them in the Press. As a fervent admirer of Virginia as a novelist already, this was very exciting to me, and my mother saw that working at the Press was something I wanted to do much more than becoming a Foreign Office or museum official. The question of a partnership could be left open for the time being. So before many days had passed, I had settled into the manager's room in the basement at 52 Tavistock Square with dreams of a publishing future to rival my great-grandfather Robert Chambers's.*

Only a month or two before I had come to know a young Oxford poet, Stephen Spender, through my sister Rosamond. Stephen told me about his close friends Wystan Auden and Christopher Isherwood. Christopher, who now lived in Berlin, had written a novel, *All the Conspirators*, which had been published by Jonathan Cape. Cape had, however, refused a second novel he had written called *The Memorial*, which was now in the hands of his agent, Curtis Brown, who was having some difficulty in finding a publisher for it. Stephen spoke of it with great enthusiasm, and when I had become part of the Hogarth Press I persuaded him to let me see a copy.

Stephen was a great maker of legends, and saw his most intimate friends and fellow-writers as a closely-knit, in fact heroic band who were out to create an entirely new literature. He wrote to me from Berlin: 'There are four or five friends who work together, although they are not all known to each other. They are W.H. Auden, Christopher Isherwood, Edward Upward and I. I only know Christopher and Wystan Auden of the other three . . . . Whatever one of us does in writing or travelling or taking jobs, it is a kind of exploration which may be taken up by the

---

* Editor of *Chambers's Journal, Chambers's Encyclopaedia* etc., a distinguished literary figure in Edinburgh life at the beginning of the nineteenth century.

other two or three.' This may have been largely Stephen's fantasy, but it was a potent stimulus to a young poet who had just taken up publishing.

As soon as I had read it, I felt the same enthusiasm, and decided to do my utmost to get Leonard and Virginia to take it on. They approached it with caution, and asked to see *All the Conspirators* before they made up their minds. Though Christopher and Stephen were filled with the direst forebodings, the result was positive, and *The Memorial* was accepted. It was published in February 1932.

I was naturally very keen to know more about the new author, and his plans for future work, and had asked Stephen to get him to write to me. A letter followed, dated 13 January, from his Berlin address in the Nollendorfstrasse:

Stephen tells me that you want me to write and let you know what I mean to do in the near future. At present I'm writing an autobiographical book, not a novel, about my education – preparatory school, public school and University. After this is finished I shall start a book about Berlin, which will probably be a novel written in diary form and semi-political. Then I have another autobiographical book in mind. And possibly a travel book. So you see, I have no lack of raw material! It is only a question of time and energy! . . . I am very glad that my novel is coming out so soon. I hope you will have more success with it than it deserves.

It seems fairly clear that the 'autobiographical book' must have been an early version of what, after many changes of title and scope, was eventually published as *Lions and Shadows*, but not until 1938. I must have written to him indicating a strong preference for the Berlin stories, because in his next letter he wrote: 'I'm sure you're prefectly right about the Berlin book. Unfortunately, however, I don't feel nearly ready to write it yet. I should probably have to get away from Berlin first. Whereas the other book is all in my head already.'

I first met Christopher when he came to London in August
1932: I had missed him when I was in Germany myself
in the earlier summer.

The young man who came into my office that morning struck
me at once by an unexpected smallness – he was only five foot
eight inches tall – and the disproportion of the large head and
dominant nose to the rest of the body. His hair was worn short – I
never knew him sport long hair – with a quiff coming over his
forehead. His expression was remarkably boyish, and remained
so as long as I knew him. There was a twinkle in his eye, which
he seemed to be able to switch on and off like an actor. I did
not see the characteristics that Auden describes in his pastiche-
Lawrence poem a few years later (1937):

> Who is that funny-looking young man so squat with a
>   top-heavy head
> A cross between a cavalry major and a rather prim landlady...
>
> With your enormous distinguished nose and your great grey
>   eyes

> Only 33 and a real diplomat already
> Our guest ambassador to the mad . . .

But it was scarcely the occasion for such observations. I wrote
of this first meeting in my diary:

> It was impossible not to be drawn to him. I was attracted
> by the warmth of his nature, and by the quality which appealed
> to me so much in *The Memorial*, an exact feeling for the deeper
> moods of our generation with its delayed war-shock and
> conviction of the futility of the old pattern of social life and
> convention; his capacity – the pressure he was under in his
> imagination – to invent the most extravagant dream-
> situations of comedy for everyone he knew, evoked a response
> in that part of me that produced the dotty fantasy plays at
> Eton; and at the same time I had fallen under the spell of his
> Berlin legend, and yet for some months after our first meeting
> our relations remained rather formal: perhaps it was the sense
> of alarm that seemed to hang in the air when his smile was
> switched off, a suspicion he seemed to radiate that one might
> after all be in league with the 'enemy', a phrase which covered
> everthing he had, with a pure hatred, cut himself off from in
> English life . . . .

In his later book, *Christopher and His Kind*, he commented
amusingly on this description:

> John's intuition was correct. Christopher *was* suspicious of and
> on his guard against this tall handsome young personage with his
> pale narrowed quizzing eyes, measured voice which might have
> belonged to a Foreign Office expert, and extremely becoming,
> prematurely grey hair – an hereditary characteristic. Seated
> behind his desk, John seemed the incarnation of authority –
> benevolent authority, but authority, none the less. What
> Christopher didn't, couldn't have realized until they knew each
> other better was that this personage contained two beings whose
> deepest interests were in conflict, an editor and a poet.

Christopher then goes on to develop his theory about my
character:

John the Editor was also in conflict with the policy of the

Hogarth Press. For he was destined to bring the writing of the thirties to birth and introduce it to the world. The Woolfs belonged to the previous generation, and their Press, despite its appearance of chic modernity, tended to represent the writing of the twenties and the teens, even the tens . . . . Meanwhile John the Poet simply wanted to write his poems . . . . He hated to waste precious time publishing books – even books by those he most admired – and he had no interest in exercising authority, however benevolent. The worst enemies of John the Poet were his friends, who wanted him to publish their works.

It was in March 1929 that Christopher had set out on one of the crucial journeys of his life: to Berlin. In *Lions and Shadows* he makes out that his chief reason was to get to know Layard, the disciple of Homer Lane, the American psychologist whose teachings were proving so exciting and revolutionary to Wystan and himself at the time; but in *Christopher and His Kind* he confesses that, though he did indeed want to meet Layard, far more important was to be introduced to the homosexual life of Berlin, of which Wystan had been giving him inflammatory accounts. He could hardly wait to be taken to such bars as The Cosy Corner, where he would be able to find Berlin boys who were ready to go to bed with foreigners, especially Englishmen, for a few marks pocket-money. He found one who suited him exactly almost at once, called Bubi, who became for him the incarnation of his dream of the 'German Boy' and the 'Blond Foreigner', who did everything he wanted in bed – chiefly by being just himself. A close attachment grew between the two of them, and though Bubi soon had to sail away from Berlin, they met again on various occasions later in Christopher's life, and always with rapturous embraces. Christopher was fortunate in this first Berlin infatuation.

It was only after we met again, briefly, in Berlin at the end of 1932, that our letters began 'Dear John' and 'Dear Christopher'. By that time I had left the Hogarth Press, perhaps as Christopher had foreseen, and gone to live in Vienna with the aim of immersing myself in poetry; though John the Editor was by no means dead. I returned to England for Christmas; and it was on my way back to Vienna that I decided to make a longer visit to Christopher in his Berlin stronghold.

Meanwhile my sister Beatrix and Christopher had met in Berlin. I cannot now remember why Beatrix was visiting Germany at that time; in any case she and Christopher immediately found a great deal in common, and became – and remained – close friends. I have a letter written from Nollendorfstrasse at the end of December, in which he says: 'Beatrix is here. I like her most awfully. Yesterday we went to see *Faust*. Gründgens played Mephistopheles as a sinister cissy and crawled up Faust's waistcoat like a caterpillar. It was an electrifying performance.' He was in great spirits because in the earlier elections the Communists had taken the lead over the Nazis in the city, and rather with his tongue in his cheek had written in the same letter: 'I shall not insult a Comrade with bourgeois Christmas Greetings, but a Revolutionary Salute for 1933 can do no harm. Rot Front.'

It was icily cold in Berlin, which seemed to me like a patient about to undergo an operation without any anaesthetic at all. I vividly remember a walk Christopher and I took one afternoon, muffled up to the eyes against the flaying wind. I wrote in my diary:

I noticed something I had not foreseen, an element, puzzling and deeply disturbing, that had been left out of the reporters' reckonings of Right versus Left, reactionary capitalism versus the working-class movement, and so on. All over the city, especially in the middle-class residential and shopping districts, huge pictures of Hitler were displayed in the failing light in windows illuminated by devout candles. The crude likenesses of the Man of Germany's Destiny, row upon row above us, were like altars dedicated to some primitive, irrational demon-cult.

Christopher had booked me a room for one month, so that I was in Berlin not only when the more or less gaga Hindenburg nominated Hitler as Chancellor at the end of January, but also for the burning of the Reichstag on 27 February. No one is likely ever to know for certain who planned this coup, but it was not the pathetic and moronic van der Lubbe who stood trial for it.

I was in a bar near the Zoo, when a friend who had been spending the evening at a cinema came in and told us 'The Reichstag's on fire!' I followed him outside, and sure enough could see the glow of flames in the east against the black sky. The immediate result was that Hitler's triumph was complete in the face of what was immediately labelled a Communist plot, and the Nazi terror was unleashed against the Communists and all the known opponents of the new regime who had not already sensed the way the wind was blowing and either gone to ground or emigrated. The press began to indulge in an orgy of Jew-baiting and sabre-rattling, and sickening stories circulated about the atrocities that were being committed in barracks and prisons against those who had been arrested. I had little doubt that most of them were true, particularly as they were exactly what had been threatened in innumerable rabid articles and pamphlets.

Christopher, who had many friends and contacts in the left-wing groups and their sympathizers, did what he could to help those in hiding and those in flight, including Gerald Hamilton (the prototype for Mr Norris). Foreigners who had no obvious affiliations were left alone, at any rate for the time being, but the frequenters of the boy-bars, many of which were being raided, passed some uneasy nights. The atmosphere became increasingly ominous, and at the beginning of April Christopher packed up a mass of his papers and letters and took them back to England, where he stayed for the rest of the month. He was still unwilling to pull up his roots, though he must have seen that the crisis could not be far off.

At that moment two things happened which made escape from Berlin much easier for Christopher. He received a bequest from an aunt who had just died, not a large bequest but very useful coming when it did. It made him feel that he could travel anywhere he liked in the world. At the same time his English friend Francis Turville-Petre reappeared in Germany. Francis (who was always known among their friends as 'The Fronny') was a disreputable homosexual who had enough money to make it simple for him to do whatever he pleased, to indulge his promiscuous tastes and live wherever he liked. Christopher was fascinated by him, though a little wary of his debauchery, and they first went off together to stay in the country together with Francis's friend Karl Giese. A young Berlin boy called Heinz was brought in to help in the household, and as the visit went on Christopher found himself more and more attracted by Heinz, went to bed with him and gradually fell in love, Heinz taking the place of a by now more or less disgraced young man called Otto. I never met Fronny, and only knew him from Christopher's talk and the fact that Wystan was writing a play about him, which started by being called *The Fronny*, then, when Christopher began to collaborate, *Where is Francis?*, and was eventually put on by the Group Theatre as *The Dog Beneath the Skin*.

Fronny now decided to live in Greece, and bought a small island called St Nicholas, in the strait between Euboea and the mainland. There he began building a house for himself, and invited Christopher (with of course Heinz) to live there with him. Christopher was strongly taken by the idea, and accepted. It seemed as good a way out of the impossible Berlin situation as any other, though it left the further future very vague. He began a diary on the eve of their departure (13 May 1933): 'It is a quarter past midnight and I have just finished packing. In eight hours I am going to leave Berlin, perhaps for ever.' In *Christopher and His Kind* he rejects this attitude as being false, saying that he doesn't believe he ever imagined the day on which he could leave Germany, and that it suggests a calm foresight of which he was incapable. But I am not convinced.

Christopher and Heinz travelled via Prague, Vienna and Budapest, then boarded a river steamer for Belgrade, where they caught the train for Athens. Francis met them there, and the next day they crossed over to the island. They had visited me in Vienna, and as Christopher was obviously attracted by it, I tried to persuade them to stay, perhaps even to settle there. But in vain: the call of the Balkans, of which Christopher had a romantic dream, was too strong. Perhaps, when they discovered how primitive living conditions were on St Nicholas and how crushing the Aegean sun was after north Germany, they wished they had. At any rate the Greek interlude was not an unmitigated success, and their discomfort and restlessness emerge pretty obviously from their letters. Christopher wrote in July: 'It is as hot as hell.

I write when Heinz makes me. Otherwise I lie on my bed and read detective stories. We are still in tents. The house won't be ready till the end of August. I'd leave almost at once if I knew where. Do write as soon as you get this.' He had also begun to worry about the danger of war breaking out, an anxiety that stayed with him during all his subsequent travels, fuelled by the alarmist reports which he read in Claud Cockburn's *The Week* – almost the only news that reached him from the outside world. 'Is there going to be a war?' he wrote in August. 'This question may well be answered before you read it. Anyhow, I can't judge anything from the scrappy paragraphs at the back of the *Athens Messenger*, whose leading articles are generally about Lord Byron, ''Sir Codrington'' or a French poet's impressions of the Aegean. I don't know how long we shall stay here. The heat obliterates all will, all plans, all decisions.' But a fortnight later the decision to leave the island was taken. For a long time the dirt, the stinging flies, the bad weather, the rowdy animal behaviour of the boys whom Francis had collected for his bed and for helping in the household chores, and the drunken sessions when the fishermen tied up at night, had been getting on Christopher's nerves. Heinz had adapted himself, with his easy nature, more rapidly to the life on the island. He joked with the boys and the workmen, even managing to carry on a kind of pidgin conversation with them, with the aid of phrase-books. Christopher, who had a strong streak of jealousy in his make-up, got into moods when he imagined that everyone was making a pass at Heinz, and the sullenness this produced in him caused Heinz to retreat into sulkiness, and suggest that Christopher should send him back to Berlin. They left for Athens on the evening of 6 September without saying goodbye to Francis, and, with rows still smouldering between them, finally took a boat for Marseilles. The rows cleared, as they were bound to, and they spent more than two more weeks in France before crossing over to England. Somehow or other Christopher managed to get a tourist visa for Heinz, and they stayed at his mother's house in Pembroke Gardens. One does not know if Christopher had already given Heinz the reckless advice to put *Hausdiener* (domestic servant) as his occupation in his passport, but in any case on this occasion it caused no trouble. Heinz was introduced to many of Christopher's friends, including my sister Beatrix to whom he became completely devoted. When the tourist visa expired, Heinz went back to Germany, though with many misgivings on Christopher's part.

III

A new chapter now unexpectedly opened in Christopher's life. Very soon after Heinz's departure, he had a telephone call from Jean Ross, whom he had met in Berlin as one of his fellow-lodgers in the Nollendorfstrasse for a time, when she was earning her living as a (not very remarkable) singer in a second-rate cabaret. She had not yet been immortalized as Sally Bowles, though Christopher must already have seen her as that character in his mind in the vast scenario of 'The Lost', out of which all his Berlin stories were eventually to be extracted and shaped.

Jean Ross now told him that she had met 'an absolutely marvellous man' who was a film director and was looking for an Englishman who could help him with the script for a film he had contracted to do for Gaumont British. She got him to read *The Memorial*, and he admired it and wanted to meet the author as soon as possible. The name of the film director was Berthold Viertel, an Austrian poet who had already directed a number of films in Hollywood. In no time at all they had met and discovered an affinity which went beyond the fact that Christopher knew all about the situation in central Europe and could discuss the film with him in German. He was hired at once, in the place of Margaret Kennedy* who had had to drop out, and they started work with considerable excitement on Christopher's part.

I got to know Viertel very well at a rather later date when I was back from Vienna in London, but I shall not describe him in detail as Christopher has given a brilliant picture of him in *Prater Violet* where he appears as Dr Friedrich Bergmann. He was short, stocky, emotional and explosive, very shrewd about the film world with a nice line in wit of his own. He was proud of his poetry, prouder than of any of the films he had directed, and much regretted that it was hardly known outside his own country. His wife, Salka, and his children were in California and so not involved in the bust-up in Austria that was taking place at that time, though in *Prater Violet* Christopher makes Dr Bergmann deeply preoccupied with it. He was not homosexual, nor did he realize that Christopher was until after the film had been finished, though the way Christopher reacted to some of his remarks about sexual habits must have made him a little suspicious. Christopher introduced him to Beatrix, whom he used later in *The Passing of the Third Floor Back*; and also fell in love with. I found him a marvellous conversationalist and a most stimulating companion to be with.

It was in the middle of the film-work that Christopher made another attempt to get Heinz into England. Almost everything went wrong. Heinz had been furnished with letters of invitation from Christopher's mother and Christopher himself, as well as a respectable sum of money. The letters were not meant to be seen by the immigration officials, but Heinz, driven into a corner by their questioning, produced them: his fatal passport description as *Hausdiener* was in front of them. Christopher, who had come down to meet the boat with Wystan, was accused of trying to deceive 'His Majesty's Immigration Service' who were not convinced that Heinz intended to work in the Isherwood household, and his own letter to Heinz was described as 'the sort of letter a man might write to his sweetheart'. In fact, they guessed

* The novelist, author of *The Constant Nymph*.

the score at once, and Heinz was sent back to Germany by the next boat. He could obviously never attempt to land in England again: it was a total disaster.

In his shame and misery Christopher was extremely unwilling to tell his friends about this scene at Harwich, though I feel that he must have written to me in Vienna, however briefly, as I was in a potential situation of the same sort, though it did not come to the boil until a few years later when Hitler annexed Austria to the German Reich. In any case the letter, if it was ever written, has disappeared. Fearing, with all too good reason, that Germany would introduce conscription, Christopher's basic aim during the next few years was to get Heinz out of Germany and settle with him somewhere beyond the reach of the Nazis. The first stop was Amsterdam. Once he had found a place for Heinz there he became much lighter-hearted, and went back to London and the final stages of the making of the film with a new determination to enjoy them. He felt he was learning an immense amount about the film world that he had always longed to know, and his obsessive war-fears receded into the background for the time being. Only now and then did he worry about Heinz's isolation, and he tried on one occasion to get me to visit him and report (paying all my expenses), but I couldn't leave Vienna at that moment, and his anxiety soon subsided.

Once he had rejoined Heinz in Amsterdam, the great debate about plans for where they were to go next – and for longer and further away – began again. Quito? Tahiti? The Seychelles? Tristan da Cunha? They rehearsed them, and many other places, and found objections to them all of one sort or another. In the end they decided to try the Canary Islands; not as far from Europe as Christopher would have liked, but being nearly part of Africa (in spite of belonging to Spain) perhaps remote enough. So, in April, they set sail from Rotterdam and reached Las Palmas on the island of Gran Canaria. They spent the next weeks in wandering about the islands, and had the luck to find a German consul who was willing to alter the disastrous *Hausdiener* in Heinz's passport to *Sprachstudent* (student of languages). In the end, in June, they chose Tenerife as the most suitable place to settle for a while, and found a pension called the

Pavillon Troika near the village of Orotava. Christopher had a strong feeling that he could work on his novel there. He had abandoned his original attempt to make it a hold-all for all the Berlin characters he wanted to write about, and decided to concentrate on Gerald Hamilton as Arthur Norris. I think, but I am not certain, that he had read Proust by then; Mr Norris has unmistakable likenesses to the Baron de Charlus: both snobs, both given to special perversions, both homosexuals (though Christopher concealed Mr Norris's homosexuality), with one important difference – Charlus was not a rogue, while Hamilton/Norris was a crook of the deepest dye. Christopher wrote to me at the end of June: 'I think my novel ought to be finished in another month. It will be dreadfully short – I'm afraid not more than 45,000. I wonder if anybody will be prepared to publish a book of that length? When it is finished, I shall begin my other Berlin book at once: nearly the whole of it is already written.' A week or two later he reported that the novel was 'exactly three quarters done. I hope to finish it on the day War was declared in 1914. It is a sort of glorified shocker; not unlike the productions of my cousin Graham Greene.'

In these letters he gives a vivid description of their life on the island:

Here, amidst the flowers, our Rousseau life goes on. Heinz has just got me to cut off all his hair. He now looks like one of the boys in a Russian film. Every morning we retire to our tables in the banana grove. H. writes letters, making at least ten copies of each. Indeed, calligraphy is dignified by him to the position of an art. One is reminded of the monks in the Middle Ages. This place is a sort of monastery, anyhow. It is run by a German of the Göring-Roman Emperor type and an Englishman who dyes his hair. The Englishman loathes women so much that he has put a barbed wire entanglement across an opening in the garden wall, to keep them out. The celebrated peak is very seldom to be seen for clouds. We have to go up it before we leave, I suppose. Heinz wheedled me up to the top of an exceedingly high mountain on Grand Canary, from which we not only saw all the kingdoms of the world, but nearly fell into the middle of them. However, for the moment, he is domesticated to a degree, and almost refuses to leave the garden, where he plays with the cats and dogs. As well as English we also study geography and I lecture him on the last fifteen years of European history out of Cole's *Intelligent Chaos*. We both eat a great deal and are immensely fat.

I have a photograph of Heinz and Christopher in the garden, among the banana trees and the hibiscus and the flowers. They look very contented. Christopher is sitting cross-legged on the grass, smiling at something Heinz is leaning out of his deck-chair to show him among papers on the ground. And I think Christopher was happy at this time, working steadily at *Mr Norris Changes Trains* (which was still at this time called 'The Lost'), once he had forced his landlord to agree not to play his gramophone until four in the afternoon.

Mr Norris was finished on 12 August. They immediately set forth on a voyage of exploration among the smaller islands, then visited Gibraltar and Spanish Morocco, then by slow stages back to settle in Copenhagen. Christopher says he can't remember why they chose Denmark, but it seemed to be a good choice as it was close to England, and most of the Danes spoke German, which made it easier for Heinz. They reached Copenhagen at the beginning of October, and there met Stephen Spender's elder brother Michael and his wife Erica, who helped them to find a lodging and proved altogether good and sympathetic friends.

A new development now occurred in Christopher's literary career. Wystan Auden sent him a play they had both worked on in the past, and which seemed likely to be put on by the Group Theatre. He and Wystan now began a collaboration on the play through letters, until Wystan himself suddenly appeared by aeroplane, and they were able to work side by side. They agreed to call it *Where is Francis?* though the eventual title *The Dog Beneath the Skin* appears to have been the suggestion of Rupert Doone, the producer.

The Auden-Isherwood plays do not, however, concern me in this narrative, as I never had anything to do with them, nor did the Hogarth Press. I enjoyed and admired *Dog Skin* (as we used to call it telegraphically amongst ourselves), *The Ascent of F.6* rather less, and *On the Frontier* scarcely at all.

IV

While in Copenhagen, Christopher worried himself to distraction about the danger of war. This worry was enormously heightened by Hitler's declaration in the middle of March that conscription was to be introduced in Germany in defiance of the Versailles Treaty. The result was that if Heinz remained abroad without registering he became automatically a criminal in the eyes of German law; and if Christopher encouraged him to remain abroad he was making himself responsible for his criminality. Heinz was an Aryan, and could not therefore throw himself on the mercy of the various organizations that were trying to help the Jews who were fleeing from Germany. It was in this situation that Christopher began seriously thinking of finding a way of Heinz changing his nationality. Unfortunately the only person who appeared to have the right contacts to explore such possibilities was Gerald Hamilton.

Meanwhile difficulties cropped up about staying in Denmark. They moved to Brussels. The acute stage of their retreat from one European country to another had begun.

Owing to the problems of having Heinz's *permis de séjour* for Belgium renewed while he was actually in Belgium, they moved over the border into Holland and found acceptable lodgings in Amsterdam, Emmastraat 24, where Heinz had stayed after the Harwich debacle. There was something about Amsterdam that calmed and reassured, and they seem to have been happy there – or at any rate as happy as people in their situation could be.

At the beginning of July I went over to Amsterdam to stay with them, not only because Christopher was always urging me to visit them, wherever they were, but also because I had urgent business to discuss with Christopher. We had for some time been planning a literary magazine, and had talked about it whenever we met and in our letters. The main idea was that it should be the magazine to publish the writings of our generation and our sympathizers, i.e. the contributors who had appeared in *New Signatures* and *New Country*,* but should also be international. I was convinced that in many countries of Europe there were new writers who felt just as we felt about the rising tide of fascism that seemed to be threatening the whole Continent, and had a similar desire to bridge the gulf between the well-educated middle classes and the still less articulate, less privileged working classes. I had met many of them in my wanderings, and already knew and admired their works. I even entertained the hope that such writers could be found in Soviet Russia, green as I was about the stifling conditions under which modern Russians worked. But I wanted to avoid writing whose whole point was to prove a political moral, such as was already appearing in *Left Review*. Christopher agreed with me whole-heartedly about this: it was a new imaginative literature we wanted to find. We also agreed that our magazine should provide a place for those long short stories, too long for magazines such as the *London Mercury*, which were often published on the Continent but were at the same

---

* Two anthologies edited by Michael Roberts. *New Signatures: poems by several hands* was published in 1932 and included work by the 'Oxford poets'. *New Country* (1933), an anthology of poetry and prose, included some poems by John Lehmann.

time too short for English publishers of novels. It was here in particular that Christopher himself was to come in, as he was already toying with the idea of breaking up what remained of 'The Lost' into separate incidents or character studies. All these points were eagerly discussed during our walks together through Amsterdam. I remember one walk which took us alongside a field where schoolboys were (in my recollection) practising football. Christopher gives a slightly different, and comic account in *Christopher and His Kind*:

Among these (teenage boys) were a few types of exotic beauty, products of Holland's colonial presence in the East Indies – nordic blond hair and peach skin with Indonesian cheekbones and liquid black equatorial eyes. At one corner of the field was a boxing-ring. The boys didn't fight, they only sparred, with a sportsman-like restraint which verged absurdly on politeness. But it was just the caressing softness with which their big leather gloves patted each other's naked bodies that Christopher found distractingly erotic. His attention would stray far from literature, and his voice, though continuing to talk about it, must have sounded like a programmed robot's: 'Oh yes, indeed I *do* agree – I think he's quite definitely the best writer in that genre, absolutely – '

As soon as I got back to London I tackled the negotiations which I had already begun with Allen Lane of the Bodley Head before leaving. We debated whether the magazine should be a quarterly or appear twice a year in hard covers like the *Yellow Book*. Eventually we decided on the latter scheme, and the name *New Writing*.

I wrote at once to Christopher to tell him the good news and that I had a contract in my pocket.

Your own contribution can be anything between 3,000 and 12,000 words long. However deeply Wystan A. may have involved himself with the Empire-builders and their film-hacks, he must not be allowed to leave for our far-flung territories without producing something. He will probably write it while you stand over him one evening. My homage to him when he comes. I think the moment has arrived for me to write to

Edward Upward myself, now that you have prepared the way. Can you give me his address? And will you find out from Stephen whether his contribution is finished, or nearly finished? Put the pen in his hand if not.

I enclosed in my letter a draft of the 'Manifesto' I wanted to appear at the beginning of the first number. On 2 September he replied from Amsterdam:

So glad the prospects for *New Writing* are so good. Do you really think paragraph four of your Manifesto is necessary at all? I only ask this tentatively. It seems to me merely the same as saying the 'vital creative work' *will* be vital. And, anyhow, the aims of the paper will be self-evident already in the contents of the first issue. It seems to me that to make any statement of your aims at all lays you open to attacks from the further and hither Left. Surely it is enough to say what you say in your other paragraphs and leave the names of the contributors to suggest the nature of the contents?

Following this piece of sound advice, I amended the 'Manifesto', though I now think not enough. Originally my idea had been that there should be a fairly informal advisory committee to assist the editor, but Christopher didn't seem very keen. In the same letter he wrote: 'Certainly I will be most honoured to sit on the advisory Committee, if you don't think my absence from England disqualifies me? But let me urge you once more to take as little notice of us all as possible, and be very autocratic. I'm sure it's better. Need you, in fact, have a formal committee at all? Why not just consult people informally, whenever you want an outside opinion?'

The rather American idea of a committee was more or less dropped. Perhaps, when he urged me to be 'very autocratic', his instinct told him that 'John the Editor' would be that anyway. But he was always full of ideas for contributions, particularly from Auden. In October, he wrote from Brussels: 'Wystan was here last week-end. He showed me some lyrics and oddments he had written for films, which I liked. And he said you should have them if you wanted them. Although some have already appeared in a film called *Coal-Face*, even the producer himself admitted that they were quite inaudible, so unless they are printed, they will be lost to mankind. I am getting on with my contribution as fast as I can.' This first extract from what remained of 'The Lost' was originally to be called 'The Kulaks'. In November a postcard arrived; 'The Kulaks are coming, hurrah, hurrah. Hope you'll like them.' I certainly did like them, very much indeed. On 16 January 1936, he wrote from Sintra, when they had moved to Portugal with Stephen and his friend after Heinz's *permis de séjour* in Belgium had run out: 'About the Kulaks: it occurs to me that maybe, if the book is to be read at all in Russia, the title conveys quite a wrong impression. Do you think I should change the family name? I could do this, of course, in proof: or maybe it could be done before the MS goes to press. What about Nowack? "The Nowacks" – Nowak, perhaps is better? Yes: "The Nowaks". (I have just been to ask Heinz, who thinks it can only be spelt Nowack: maybe you could check up on this?)' Surprisingly enough, the story *was* read in Russia, where it appeared in a little paperback all by itself, titled (in Cyrillic) 'НОВАК'. In the same letter, he went on: 'What are you writing now? Am very busy on my novel. I will try and do something for number three. There is another section of 'The Lost' ready – about an English girl who sings in a Berlin cabaret, but I hardly think it would suit the serious tone of *New Writing*. It's rather like Anthony Hope: 'The Dolly Dialogues'. It is an attempt to satirize the romance-of-prostitution racket. Good heter stuff.'

This was, of course, the genesis of the eventually far-famed *Sally Bowles*. He was not, however, satisfied with it. When he had only seen the contents list of the first number of *New Writing*, he wrote from Sintra: 'we are all very much excited about *New Writing* . . . . I'm afraid I couldn't get the proposed story ready for the *next* number. It is finished after a fashion but there's something radically wrong with it at present: it must be thought over.' More than that, he wanted to see what Edward Upward thought about it. And there was also, crucially, the need to get the approval of the real-life Sally Bowles (Jean Ross).

By the end of April, *New Writing* No.1 had arrived in

Sintra. Christopher hailed it with enthusiasm:

> I must say, I think it is very handsome and one of the
> best six shillings–worth I have ever seen. I haven't read
> everything yet, of course. Yours, which I turned to first, seems
> admirable. One of your most successful works . . . . I liked also
> very much Plomer's contribution* and that brilliant story by
> Chamson§ ('My Enemy'), which makes one feel that a real
> artist can write about absolutely anything and still produce all
> the correct reflections about fascism, nationalism etc. in the
> reader's mind: a very trite observation, but it always comes as
> a fresh surprise.

He urged me to publish Edward Upward's 'The Railway
Accident' in No.2, as he thought it 'one of the most magnificent
pieces of narrative prose produced since the war', and would need
very little bowdlerization; but this plan fell through, chiefly, as
far as I remember, owing to the author's then reluctance. And
he went on: 'Look here, if you'd like some stuff for Number Two,
I could send you some of my Berlin Diary. About five thousand
words. But don't have it if you don't want. It is only mildly (heter)
dirty and chiefly about my landlady, fellow-lodgers, pupils, etc.'

I did want it (and published it in fact in No.3), but the
problems of the longer story had to be settled first. In October
he wrote to me in Vienna from London: Sally Bowles has
unexpectedly passed Edward Upward – so I am sending it to
you. If you like it and want to publish, we must somehow get
the consent of the original, who is at present abroad, otherwise
the risk of an action is too great for us to take.'

The risk of a libel action was not the only problem as far
as I was concerned. I was fascinated by it, and certainly didn't
think it was too frivolous for our magazine; but it was long, too
long even by the standards of New Writing, and I certainly didn't
want to divide it into two. More than that, I was worried about
the abortion episode, and was nervous whether our printers – in
the climate of those days – would pass it. I explained my doubts

* The novelist, William Plomer. His contribution was called 'Notes on
a visit to Ireland'.
§ The French novelist, André Chamson.

to Christopher. He wrote back from Brussels in January 1937: 'About Sally, you know I'm doubtful, though quite open to conviction. It seems to me that Sally, without the abortion sequence, would just be a silly little capricious bitch. Besides, what would the whole thing lead up to? And down from? The whole idea of the study is to show that even the greatest disasters leave a person like Sally essentially unchanged.'

After this sensible letter I luckily gave up the rather half-hearted attempt to persuade Christopher to cut Sally. Meanwhile, however, Jean Ross had given her permission, and *Sally Bowles* was published, with what struck me as considerable courage, fortified by the success they had had with *Mr Norris Changes Trains*, as a separate little book by Leonard and Virginia Woolf at the Hogarth. It was eventually included in *Goodbye to Berlin* with the other pieces rescued from 'The Lost'. One more of these pieces, 'The Landauers', was first printed in *New Writing*.

In *Christopher and His Kind* Christopher makes a rather too generous acknowledgement to me: 'Christopher would soon owe a great debt to John. His continuing demand for material forced Christopher to do what he was stupidly unwilling to do – publish the rest of his Berlin writings as disconnected fragments, suitable in length for the magazine, instead of trying to fit them into a stodgy plot-ridden story. Thus John became responsible for the informal form of *Goodbye to Berlin*.'

Some years later, in an interview in America, Christopher offered a rather more sophisticated apologia for this 'informal form'. 'The Lost', he said,

would have been like Balzac's *Splendeurs et Misères des Courtisanes* – very complicated, all sorts of absurd contrivances to bring it all together, hundreds of characters . . . . And then I fell upon the understanding that as far as I was concerned you can get just the same effect by little broken bits of something, that the gaps are not worth filling in, that's all just plotting. And so what I did was I took up all the broken bits and put them into *Goodbye to Berlin* just as slivers of something. And you got just the same effect, that you've met a whole world.

I have a distinct recollection that Christopher let me see what was left over from the operations, the pieces left on the cutting-room floor so to speak – and some of it was very fascinating – and I have never known whether he kept these fragments or destroyed them when he destroyed his diaries.

V

In the autumn of 1935 Heinz's *permis de séjour* problems had become urgent again: he couldn't get the Belgian authorities to grant him a longer stay after a visa he had obtained in Luxemburg lapsed. It so happened that Stephen and his ex–Guards friend 'Jimmy Younger' came to Brussels just at that time. They agreed to go to Portugal with Christopher and Heinz and try living *à quatre* out there. So at the beginning of December the four of them set sail in a Brazilian boat that would drop them in Lisbon on its way to Rio. On 17 December they reached the mouth of the Tagus, and within twenty-four hours had found a house they liked at Sintra, and stayed there for some months. The experiment of living *à quatre* did not last very long, but long enough for them all to get caught in a gambling fever at the Casino in Estoril. Christopher wrote to me in March:

The gambling rumours are, alas, true. But not under this roof. We go to Estoril, which is a taxi-ride, and so mildly, very mildly, deterrent. We don't really do it very often but when we do we lose generously. Stephen parted with nearly twenty pounds, I believe. Worse, we have been dabbling in the occult sciences, at the house of two lady anthroposophists: Tarot pack, Rudolf Steiner and all that. I continue to like this place. It is very quiet, but is really beautiful, and it is so restful living in the country for a change. Of course, the future is as vague for us as for everybody else. But H. seems to have at any rate a certain hold here. There are very few Germans, good bad or indifferent, in this part of the country, so there is no alien problem and no one seems to care much. He loves the place, which is nice. I do wish you could come, but it is hardly on the aeroplane route: though you *can* fly here, and I can see the aerodrome where you would land if you did from this window.

In later letters he writes: 'All remains set fair in this garden of Eden . . .' and 'This country is marvellously beautiful, all wooded mountains and ruined baroque palaces, and the people are charming. We are looking round for a real house with a big garden. Already we have a small dog, a cock and six hens. Soon we are getting rabbits, and later a cockatoo, a peacock and a monkey.'

The name of the small dog was Teddy, and he made messes, which Heinz never seemed to mind clearing up. In fact, he loved all the animals, and they were the centre of his life, as they had made his happiness in Tenerife. While Heinz played with them, Christopher struggled to write 'Paul is Alone', which he gave up in May, to concentrate on the book which, after many changes of scope, was to become *Lions and Shadows*. Wystan came over for a visit, and encouraged by what Christopher called the 'non-failure' of *Dog Skin*, they set about writing a new play, *The Ascent of F.6*, which was to be more truly a collaboration than the earlier play.

In the middle of this a 'politely menacing note' arrived from Leonard Woolf: 'I hear a rumour that Methuens are publishing a book by you. I presume that this must be a mere rumour in view of the fact that you have agreed to give us the first offer of your next novel, and that you told me that you would probably be sending it to us to consider in the autumn?'

But it *was* true that Christopher had signed up for a new novel with Methuen. He says in *Christopher and His Kind* that he had done it in a fit of pique because Virginia Woolf had not invited him to meet her. But with my experience of the way agents plotted to get promising authors away from the Hogarth Press who had started them off, I can almost hear Christopher being told that the Hogarth was far too small an outfit ever to do him justice in sales etc. and that he needed the expertise of a bigger and more powerful firm . . . . In any case he did publish *Lions and Shadows* and *Goodbye to Berlin* with the Hogarth, on the technical grounds that neither of them was a novel. And by then he had met Virginia, and been utterly fascinated by her. By then, too, I was back at the Hogarth.

During those months in Portugal, Christopher spent a considerable amount of time and trouble in helping me in various ways with the future numbers of *New Writing*. He kept his friends up to the mark with their promises of contributions, and gave shrewd advice about pieces that were sent to us. He also gave unstinting advice about my own work. I had written a long short story about Vienna and he suggested various improvements. When I sent him the emended version, in July, he wrote me a long letter about what it still needed done to it.

I have already been carefully through the story twice. I think it is enormously improved, and obviously the Lane reader was an idiot to refuse it, as it is certainly one of the best contributions I have seen so far. At the same time, at the risk of making you quite desperate, I must say I should like you to rewrite it just once more! The idea is so extraordinarily good and rich and fruitful of suggestions that it should be worked out to the full and no pains spared to develop it. Already it has ceased to be merely an anecdote and become something symbolic, which of course is what you want; but I feel that, in following the working out of the fable, you haven't paid enough attention to the characters. For instance, I don't think Rains himself is clear enough. I should like him much more personal, even a bit satirized perhaps. And then his relations with Rudi are not made as interesting as they might be. I know you want to keep off the homosexual note; but surely it is just this kind of homosexuality, this semi-erotic interest in the working classes, which is so profoundly significant . . .   unless you make the relationship between the two of them more vivid and lively, you hardly explain why Rains took so much trouble to find Rudi. And it is just this idea which contains the whole allegory which the story is meant, as I see it, to convey. Again, another frightfully important symbolic counter is the dead writer whose works Rains is investigating. You say that Rains' attitude towards this writer was changed by his experiences in Vienna, but you don't go into details. This seems to me a profoundly exciting idea, and one which goes to the roots of the whole business . . . .

He ended up by saying that 'if you really worked out all the implications of this subject you would have ceased to write a short story and have written a short novel. Very well, so much the better. It is a novel, and the longer you make it the better it will be . . . .'

I did eventually follow this profound and sympathetic advice, and enlarged and re-wrote the story once more, and had it published as a novel under the title *Evil Was Abroad*. I have no recollection of what Christopher thought of the final version, but I was immensely touched and impressed by the trouble he took about it – more than I remember any editor taking with a work of mine, before or since.

Meanwhile, Hitler had taken the fatal decision to reintroduce conscription for German subjects, which caused almost hysterical anxiety in the Sintra household. They were well aware that the Germans knew exactly where in Portugal young subjects affected by the new decrees could be found. In the last days of June the blow fell. They came back from a lunch-party in Estoril to find a letter from the German Consulate on the hall table, instructing Heinz Neddermayer to report in the near future to get his orders for military service. The misery of the next few weeks was aggravated by the outbreak of the Spanish Civil War.

It soon became clear to Christopher that the only hope of saving Heinz from return to Germany and military service, was for him to change his nationality and become the subject of a country outside Europe, though even that was not necessarily safe. Many of their friends in Portugal told them that it was an illusory hope. Nevertheless, Christopher set in train the moves to obtain a Mexican passport for Heinz which ended so fruitlessly and ignominiously a few months later.

A large sum of money had to be obtained in order that various Mexican officials should be bribed. Christopher persuaded his rather reluctant mother to produce this money from family funds. He sent it to a lawyer Gerald Hamilton had found for him, who, Gerald said, could handle the Mexicans. From my own experience of Gerald's habits, there is not the slightest doubt in my mind that most of the money went into Gerald's own pocket. I was astonished by Christopher's trust in Gerald, though he confesses he had grave doubts from time to time; he refused to admit to himself that Gerald was capable of diddling his closest friends. I am convinced that Christopher was his dupe all along, and that the various manoeuvres of alleged Mexican agents and the promises that were made to him that the passport would arrive any minute were eyewash. It is tragic to think that one of the most generous instincts in Christopher's character, his loyalty to his friends, was taken such cynical advantage of.

When the Mexican conspiracy was started, Christopher's mother insisted that he should leave Portugal and be nearer at hand in northern Europe. So they returned to Belgium, sad though Heinz was to leave all the animals and the garden life behind. I remember going to see them in Brussels at the end of September; we had not met for nearly fifteen months. I burst into his hotel bedroom, and was astonished to see Heinz lying in the big double bed and Christopher in a tiny camp-bed alongside. Heinz was not by any means a big man.

Early in 1937, Christopher went to Paris to see Wystan off to the Spanish War, and while he was there he discussed his problems with the writer James Stern and his wife Tania, whom he had met for the first time in Sintra. Tania, a very intelligent and practical person, suggested that it would do Heinz good psychologically if he were to learn a trade, and said she knew a silversmith who would be prepared to teach him. So, after some difficulty in getting a *permis de séjour* for Heinz they moved to Paris. For Christopher the special attraction was the presence in Paris of Cyril Connolly, his American first wife Jean, and his friend-disciple Tony Bower. Cyril had already declared himself a keen admirer of *The Memorial*, *Mr Norris Changes Trains* and 'The Nowaks'.

Christopher had not been in one of his best moods when I visited him in Brussels in September-October. I went to Brussels again, however, in January, and soon found that my fears of an obstacle having protruded itself in our friendship could be utterly discarded. We were as intimate as we had ever been, and whatever tension there had been in my imagination during the earlier visit had vanished like the morning mist. We talked and talked, all day and half the night, discussing the Heinz problem, the books and plays he was engaged on, Wystan's imminent departure for Spain, Stephen's marriage to Inez Pearn, and the future that now looked so rosy for *New Writing* with two numbers out and both successes. We went out in the evening to the bars and (mildly) debauched ourselves, still talking furiously all the time. In the morning, he gave me the typescript of 'The North-West Passage', in the last stages of its transformation into *Lions and Shadows* but not yet finished, and I retired to a café to read it. He was all keyed up to know my opinion, and I could report to him that I thought it was going to be one of his most original works.

At the beginning of April Christopher left Brussels for London, probably on business to do with the Group Theatre. While he was at Pembroke Gardens, he managed to fall ill with an ulcerated mouth, due apparently to a tooth that had been incompletely extracted. He ran a high fever and caused his doctor considerable anxiety. While he was in bed, on 17 April, Wystan, who appears to have been delayed leaving for Spain, telephoned him from Paris. Heinz had got into some slightly mysterious trouble with the French police, by sheer bad luck. I had gone back to Austria, and Christopher wrote to me there from Luxemburg:

I have been ill, and while I was in bed Heinz managed to get himself into difficulties with the French police, mild difficulties really, but they were exaggerated wildly, Heinz being a Boche, and used as an excuse to refuse to prolong his *permis de séjour* in France. His troubles had also been communicated to the Belgian authorities, who, as you know, aren't exactly pro-German either, and the net result is that we can't return to Belgium either, except for three or four days. We are, therefore on the advice of our lawyer, waiting here until the Mexican business has been put through (which really looks like being very soon: the papers are in Bruxelles and they are only waiting for the return of the Mexican Ambassador, who is away) because as soon as Heinz has ceased to be a Boche it seems that the Belgian authorities will regard his case more leniently. Tiresome, isn't it?

It was a great deal more than tiresome, as Christopher knew in his heart of hearts. He must have realized that the trap was closing in on Heinz. I have no personal knowledge of the last moves that led to the final disaster, but in *Christopher and His Kind* he blames himself for his fatalistic attitude towards what was happening. The Luxemburg authorities had no doubt received from their French colleagues the latest list of German undesirables, and informed Heinz that he could not stay under their protection any longer. The only thing to do was to apply for another Belgian visa, but that could only be done, in the time available, in Germany. Heinz must therefore take the risk of going to the nearest German town, Trier as it happened, where there was a Belgian Consulate. So Christopher left for Brussels, and the lawyer drove Heinz to Trier. Everything appeared to be going smoothly, the visa was obtained, but at the last moment the German police struck. Heinz was arrested as a draft-evader and a criminal who had indulged in homosexual practices. Christopher had told him to put all the blame on him if the worst occurred, and plead guilty to the least culpable of homosexual offences, mutual masturbation, with a degenerate Englishman who had seduced him. The court accepted this plea, and Heinz was sentenced to six months in prison, followed by a year's labour service and two years in the Army. He was lucky not to be sent to a concentration camp, as many homosexuals had already been sent. Christopher did not see Heinz again until after the war, but was left with a feeling of profoundest misery, frustration and guilt.

From Brussels he wrote to me a few days later:

As the result of a lot of complicated misfortunes and idiotic decisions which I simply haven't the heart to describe to you just now, Heinz is sitting in prison at this moment charged with attempted desertion from the army and moral offences. If he is lucky, he'll get off with three to four months, followed by camp and army service.

There's nothing I can do to help, except pay for cigarettes and extra nice food.

I feel that, at this time, you are one of the very few people I would like to be with. Would you mind if I came to Vienna in the fairly near future – in a week or two, perhaps?

Write to me at 70 Square Marie-Louise, as soon as you can, about this. I have to go to London for a day or two, and Paris after, but shall be back early next week. Best love.

But Christopher did not come to Vienna, though I would have been very happy to see him there. He and Wystan had just been commissioned to write a book about the Far East and the Chinese-Japanese war, and Christopher came to realize that a great deal of work had accumulated that would have to be dealt with before they left. In a letter apologizing for having been unable to make up his mind about a visit to Vienna, he listed it all:

If possible, I want to get the new play, *On the Frontier*, produced before Christmas. Then there is 'The North-West Passage', which I finished this morning: it will mean lots of business interviews and proof-correcting and what not. Then I'd like, if possible, to write all the remaining fragments of 'The Lost' before we sail, so that my Berlin life is finally tidied up, all ready to be audited before the Judgment Seat. You shall certainly have some of it for *New Writing*. Then there are my lectures to be prepared, on the New Drama (!). And I really ought to try and earn some more cash, with the films. So you see . . . .

Meanwhile, in that autumn of 1937, delicate moves were being made both by myself and the Hogarth Press to rejoin forces. I was anxious for *New Writing* to find a new home, as my contract with Lawrence & Wishart had run out,* and Leonard and Virginia were fed up with all the work that running the Press by themselves had landed them with. Approaches of a friendly and forgiving nature were made on both sides, with the result that it was decided that I should start with them again, and become a partner in 1938. I kept Christopher informed of the progress of the plan, and he was delighted to think that the Press might once again present itself as the publisher of *our* books. He had managed to persuade Leonard and Virginia to publish Edward Upward's novel, *Journey to the Border*, and they were going to have his now fully revised and completed *Lions and Shadows*. What was more important, Virginia made belated advances to him to wipe out the largely imaginary neglect he had felt before, and he was completely conquered. He wrote to me from Pembroke Gardens in November:

Edward's book is being published by the Hogarth in early spring. This after a terrific putsch on my part. There was a wonderful dinner party given by the Woolfs to the Upwards, a great success. Virginia is really the nicest woman I know: she was so nice to Mrs U. Elizabeth Bowen came in afterwards, so Edward got a real glimpse of Bloomsbury, and quite enjoyed it, in his chilly way.

Am in the middle of 'The Landauers' and hope to have it for the date we fixed, but, at present, work hs held up by letter-writing and lecturing. I have just got back from Oxford, that doleful town.

* The publishing of *New Writing* had been transferred from The Bodley Head to Lawrence & Wishart.

VI

The plan for Christopher and Wystan to write a travel book together about some Far Eastern country had been worked out between Faber and Random House, the publishers of their plays in England and America, before the invasion of Manchuria by the Japanese. But the outbreak of war between China and Japan gave the whole project a new angle. A war of their own! That was now the bait. Not the front stalls of the Spanish War, so crowded already with celebrities, from Malraux and Hemingway to their own English friends. Wystan had been there already, and had returned to England with mixed feelings, his deep-seated Christian convictions offended by the burning of churches on the Republican side. They were nearly coralled into a visit just before they set off for China, but the visas did not arrive in time and they had to catch their boat. After a noisy farewell party in London attended by most of their friends, they caught the boat-train for Dover on 19 January, and after spending that night in Paris, embarked two days later on the *Aramis* in Marseilles. There was a great deal of publicity about their departure, with cameras at Victoria, which Christopher thoroughly enjoyed. Their plan was to make Hong Kong their headquarters, from which to arrange their journeys into China and the war-zone. On 24 February Christopher wrote to me from the University in Hong Kong, where they were staying with the Vice-Chancellor, D.J. Sloss, whom he said might be Edgar Wallace's twin brother.

The hospitality here is astonishing. Everybody very kind, and everything done for you quite as a matter of course . . . .

Am longing to see *New Writing*. Could a copy come out here? This address holds certainly till the end of May, if not later. And thank you so much for collating the typescripts of the 'Lost' stories. I still don't know if America has taken the book: only that *Harper's Bazaar* has offered to make *Sally Bowles* into a serial. Do keep me posted on all the latest Hogarth Press and *Daylight** developments. If I am killed in China, I'd like my name on the notepaper just the same, with a cute little black cross against it! I suppose the Spender gossip must wait till we return. God knows what dimensions it'll have reached by then!

Delighted to hear that Electra is going well. Give Peggy my dearest love. I hear from another source that Viertel is going to produce Rosamond's play. Another thing we'll miss!

Our plans are taking shape. Next Saturday, we cross for one night to Macao, the Portuguese colony which provides stolid Hong Kong with its night-life: there are even special late boats, leaving there at three in the morning. On Sunday afternoon, we return here, pack, and leave early on Monday for Canton by river-boat. There are no Jap troops round Canton, but the Jap planes bomb the railway every afternoon, and drop bombs all round the city. On the whole, people say, they've behaved well, in so far as they've stuck to military objectives and avoided actually slaughtering civilians. The chief danger is that they're really bad shots. We plan to stay in Canton two or three days. Then we meet a rather sinister Col. Lawrence sort of man named Carlton, who drives a lorry

---

* *Daylight: European Arts and Letters, Yesterday, Today, Tomorrow*, a magazine which first came out in 1941, published by the Hogarth Press.

backwards and forwards between Canton and Hankow, for a cigarette firm. The road is rather problematical, floods, broken bridges, etc., and the journey may take as much as ten days. Once at Hankow, we'll be in the middle of things. Most of the government is there, and we can get the necessary passes and introductions for a visit to one or other of the fronts. Also, we hope to see the new British Ambassador, whom we met for a few minutes while he was passing through here. He is a very live wire, and ready to be helpful. Also, he reads Auden and enjoyed *Sally Bowles*. After the war stuff, we may go up the Yangtze as far as Chungking, as the gorges are said to be magnificent. Then back, probably, to Hankow, whence there is an air-service to Hong Kong. Our second journey, after suitable convalescence, will be to Shanghai, Pekin, and possibly Japan. But we may do Japan later, *en route* for America. There is also the possibility of travelling down into Yun-nan, to see the new university which is opening there in the Spring. Ambiguity Empson is to be one of the professors. He's here now and we see him a lot. Do you know him? He's nice.

Hong Kong is the ugliest town in the loveliest harbour I have ever seen. A cross between Manchester and Buxton. The view from the peak of the island is a real Chinese painting, with junks and little rock-garden crags embedded in a green plate-glass sea. Yesterday evening, we dined with the Governor, and Sir Victor Sassoon showed us a coloured film he had taken himself, of the Governor's arrival in Hong Kong. Wystan, who is having a Proust fit, enjoyed himself hugely. I was slightly more acid, as I am suffering slightly from a mild local variety of dysentery known as 'Hong Kong Dog'. Most of the big nobs here are inclined to be pro-Chinese; and you can talk about the Communist troops in even the most polite society without a shudder. So much for the ideology of Business when its interests are really threatened!

Please go on writing, as we shall hope for a bumper post to console us on our return here. And give my love to all the gang, with our news, to any who are interested.

Wystan asks to be remembered. Remembrances to your Mother.

The reference to Peggy's Electra is to my sister's performance in O'Neill's *Mourning Becomes Electra*, one of her greatest triumphs. Rosamond's play was *No More Music*, the only play she ever wrote, which was put on for one night in this season. The new British Ambassador was Sir Archibald Clark Kerr (later Lord Inverchapel), whom I got to know rather well during the war when he came on leave to England, and was able to introduce to the British intellectuals of our generation. He called Christopher and Wystan 'the Poets', and though the pretence was that he was unaware that they visited the semi-erotic bath-houses on their free afternoons, I am pretty certain he did know, whether he had them followed or not, and didn't care tuppence. The important thing was that they didn't bring the masseurs back to the Embassy. The story of their explorations of the war zones is told in their *Journey to a War*, with some additions in *Christopher and His Kind*. They must have seemed an odd pair of war-correspondents, with Wystan in his perpetual carpet-slippers (because of his corns) and woollen cap, and Christopher with his beret and oversized riding-boots trying to look the part but hurrying to take shelter whenever danger threatened.

'The Poets' made their return journey via North America, having, by a luck fluke, got open visas for the USA while they were in Shanghai. After a brief glimpse of Japan, they sailed from Yokohama to Vancouver, Christopher amazed at the welcoming attitude of the immigration officials, whom, as a class, he had, after his European experiences, come to consider prime examples of the 'enemy'. They headed for New York, where they found George Davis, novelist and literary editor, awaiting them. George Davis was, it seemed to them, a miracle worker, providing them at once with everything they asked for, including dollars from their travel articles which he had already sold. He produced an even greater miracle for Christopher, by finding for him exactly the kind of American boy he had dreamed of. In *Christopher and His Kind* he says he asked, recklessly, for 'a beautiful blond boy, about eighteen, intelligent, with very sexy legs'. In a trice, the boy was produced, full of admiration for the Englishman who had just returned from exotic adventures. Christopher calls him 'Vernon', and in the excitement of arriving in New York became infatuated with him. He became the representative 'American Boy' in Christopher's mind, as Bubi had so many years before become the 'German Boy' for him. From the moment of first meeting, 'Vernon' occupied the place in Christopher's emotional life that had been left vacant when Heinz had been wrested from him. When he returned to England, 'Vernon' continued to haunt him, and became the image, the symbol of the America he thought more and more of returning to. Auden has left it on record that he and Christopher decided to live in America definitively during this visit; but though that may have been true of Wystan, the impression I had of Christopher's state of mind during the following months of Munich and after does not lead me to believe that he was anything like as decided.

On 17 July they reached London after the 'nine days' wonder' of their visit to New York. They were just in time to see Beatrix in her one-night-only performance in the Group Theatre production of Cocteau's *La Voix Humaine*.

VII

One of the first things Christopher did was to drive down with me to the Isle of Wight, where my mother was staying in my godmother Violet's Totland Bay house while Violet was away in France. I had thought that during the drive Christopher would be able to tell me all about his adventures in China, but what in fact happened was that I encouraged him to tell me more of the great fantastic serial, of the utmost obscenity and ingenuity, which he had begun during our evenings together the year before; and once he had started there was no stopping him, episode after episode rolled out in the wildest flow of invention as if it had all been prepared and clear in his mind long before. It could never have been written down, at any rate in those days, but I was staggered by the story-telling skill he put into this anarchic fantasy, more extravagant than anything in the Mortmere saga. Alas, that was the last occasion I was ever to listen to it, though he could have started it again at any moment. Nor was there any reason why it should ever end – his own private soap opera.

That corner of the island was full of nostalgic memories

for both of us. Before the war, right up to 1915, the whole Lehmann family had taken its summer holidays at Totland, and Beatrix and I had explored the heather downs and Alum Bay together. For Christopher, Freshwater Bay, only a few miles away, was partly the scene of the action of *All the Conspirators* and the visits of Edward Upward, Wystan Auden and Hector Wintle* way back in the twenties.

I have various pictures of him in my memory during that week-end, though an excellent photograph of him on the cliff-walk, with the sea foam just visible far below in the camera's finder, looking absurdly boyish, chubby and grinning, was ruined in the developing. Other pictures of him come to mind with extraordinary vividness: one, of him pacing up and down the tiny lawn of Violet's house, with a glimpse of the Solent through the trees, discussing China with me or debating the title for his Berlin book; another, of him sitting at the lunch-table, or after dinner in the little drawing-room, endlessly lecturing my mother – to her fascination and delight – in the gentle, bright persuasive way that was his own patent for young or old disciples, explaining China, discussing what he had seen in America, describing Wystan and the lives of his friends, blissfully ignoring the indiscretions that I saw popping up like cowpats in his path – but just, it seemed by a miracle, avoiding them.

We set off, almost as soon as we arrived and I had introduced Christopher to mother, for a long walk over the downs. We discussed everything in the world that interested us – really the first chance to do so since February. Chiefly, the plans for the Hogarth Press, which I had by then rejoined, plans for *New Writing* and of course our own books. Christopher revealed himself again as a masterly describer of his unfinished and unbegun novels. I had not been so fascinated, listening to his description of the next novel, to be founded on the years of exile with Heinz, since I heard him describe, in a low *lokal* in Antwerp, with the utmost vividness, the never written novel 'Paul is Alone'. Perhaps it was because the story was so alive in all its details before he put pen to paper that the novels seemed sometimes so boring

---

* A friend of Isherwood's from Repton.

to him when he came to the hard work of writing them down.

I told him how, in the first two holidays of the war, Beatrix and I had convinced ourselves that we had spotted German spies as we clambered over the heather, and lying out of sight (we thought) on our bellies in the hollows, tracked their movements for hours together. We kept our discoveries a secret from our two elder sisters and our parents – perhaps because we felt that they'd laugh at us. This delighted Christopher, who kept on urging me to remember more, and added some fantastic strokes from his own imagination.

During the few months that elapsed between their return from China and their departure for America, Christopher and Wystan were occupied in finishing *Journey to a War*, for which purpose they retired to Brussels at the end of the year. They also saw the first night of *On the Frontier* at the Arts Theatre in Cambridge, with Lydia Lopokova in the lead. Christopher writes of the occasion in *Christopher and His Kind*: 'The first-night audience was friendly. It laughed whenever it could and treated the rest of the play with polite respect. *On the Frontier* wasn't a harrowing disaster; it passed away painlessly.' Equally, it was not a rousing success; less successful than either of its two predecessors. This, I think, was almost certainly because its theme was far too much of a reality in the minds of the audience at that particular moment in history to be dealt with in oblique fantasy: Munich was only a few weeks past.

When Christopher thought of the plans for the coming return to America – which had now been fixed for 19 January – 'Vernon' loomed large. But it would be wrong to think that this delectable image had blotted out the memory of Heinz. He thought of Heinz continually; but what could he do? He did persuade me to make a detour by Berlin the next time I drove from Vienna to London, and I succeeded in getting in touch with Heinz. I was able to report to Christopher that he seemed in good fettle, working off the year of *Arbeitsdienst* to which he had been sentenced by helping put up a new building on the Potsdamerplatz, much tougher and more reliant than before and without any rancour towards Christopher. Very soon after he met a girl he fell in love with and married. It was an

encouraging meeting, and helped Christopher to slough off much
of the guilt-feeling which had oppressed him. They continued
to correspond until the war made it too difficult.

Not unnaturally, the alarms and preparations for war which
preceded Munich drove Christopher into a panic frenzy: he had
been waiting for it to break out for five years, and here it was
just round the corner, with gas-masks being issued and all. We
became very close, seeing one another every day and feverishly
discussing the news as the papers came out. I made enquiries
about what we could do in war-time from friends in the Foreign
Office, and we agreed that we would offer ourselves for
propaganda work. 'If we've got to have a war', Christopher said,
'I'm going to see we have a good war, anyway.' His mother
and his brother Richard left for Wales, and settled that if the war
actually broke out they would stay there, and close the house in
Pembroke Gardens. So I suggested that in that case he must come
and share my flat with me; a proposal that, I think, pleased and
touched him, to judge from what he wrote in *Down There on a
Visit*. And then the meetings at Bad Godesberg and Munich
happened, and France and Britain connived at the betrayal of
the Czechs with Hitler and Mussolini. In the almost hysterical
mood of relief that swept the country, some of us felt as much
shame and foreboding as relief. As we read the latest editions
of the evening papers, I said to Christopher bitterly: 'Well, that's
the end of Europe as we wanted it', and voiced the fear that unless
further betrayals were imminent Munich could only mean the
postponement of war and not its avoidance. And in an unguarded
moment Christopher replied: 'That doesn't matter any more to
me: I shall be in America.'

But I find it difficult to believe, even at that moment, that
he had decided to become an American citizen rather than make
another, longer visit. He had said that when it came to the point
he would be guided by Wystan's decision; but I was not to know
that Wystan had decided on emigration – if what he has since
asserted is true.

Whatever conclusion they had come to in their private talks,
they had still to find the money for the journey. They therefore
proposed to me that they should collaborate on another travel

book, and that it should be called *Address Not Known*, and be published by the Hogarth Press. They arrived one morning at the Hogarth offices in Mecklenburgh Square and signed the contract. At the same time Wystan agreed to let the Hogarth publish his next book of poems – this was part of the plot Christopher and I had hatched to make the Hogarth the main publishing house for all of us. I gave Wystan a cheque from my private funds, not large, but it solved the most urgent financial problems for him. But *Address Not Known* was never written; and when Wystan's new book of poems was announced in Hogarth advance publicity some time later, T.S. Eliot wrote a polite letter to inform me that Faber had contractual rights to it. Over a good-tempered lunch he convinced me that he was right. In gentlemanly fashion Fabers paid me back what I had advanced to Wystan, and that was the end of the grand plot. I felt a bit of a fool, but I think that Christopher had acted in ignorance of the true situation. I am not sure that the same could be said of Wystan, who sent me a remarkably irritating cable from New York saying that he was helpless to sort things out.

There was one other matter, entirely personal, in which I did what I could to extricate Christopher from an erotic tangle in which he had quite recklessly involved himself. During the months before their departure he was beseiged by a large number of young men whose one idea was to have an affair with the celebrity who had written the Berlin stories. Christopher did nothing to discourage them, revelling in his success, and got himself in so deep with at least one of them that he more or less promised to take him to New York. How this was to be squared with 'Vernon' I never gathered, but he appealed to me – I knew and liked the young man – to help him get out of the mess. This uncomfortable task I took on, as best I could, and earned Christopher's gratitude but no one else's.

VIII

After many, and rather tearful, goodbyes as the boat-train left London, they sailed, on 19 January as planned, on the French liner the *Champlain*. They almost immediately ran into storms, and arrived in New York in a blizzard, and Christopher's enthusiasm for the New World plummeted: what greeted them was so starkly different from the picture they had been building up all the time in their minds, in spite of the presence of their friends to welcome them. Christopher never took to New York, as he had hoped, but Wystan, in the first few months, had the transforming experience of meeting the young man, Chester Kallman, who was to remain his closest friend for the rest of his life. Wystan and Christopher took an apartment together on East 81st Street, but Christopher was already dreaming of California. At the beginning of May he and 'Vernon' set off for the Golden West in a long-distance bus, so that they could see as much of America as possible on the way. Just before he left, he sent me his first long letter:

As soon as I'm in Hollywood, I plan to write a piece for

you about New York. I have quite a lot to say about it.
Oh God, what a city! The nervous breakdown expressed in
terms of architecture! The skyscrapers are all Father-fixations.
The police-cars are fitted with air-raid sirens, specially designed
to promote paranoia. The elevated railway is the circular
madness. The height of the buildings produces visions similar to
those experienced by Ransom in *F.6*, which reminds me that
F.6 is being done, quite grandly, sometime in August. We have
written a new ending, and, altogether, I hope it may be a real
success.

This was not the first time, nor the last, that they wrote a new
ending: they never seemed to get it to their liking, or their
changing view of its intention. He went on:

I myself am in the most Goddamawful mess. I have
discovered, what I didn't realize before, or what I wasn't till
now, that I am a pacifist. And now I have to find out what
that means, and what duties it implies. That's one reason why
I am going out to Hollywood, to talk to Gerald Heard and
Huxley. Maybe I'll flatly disagree with them, but I have to
hear their case, stated as expertly as possible. And I have to get
ready to cope with the war situation, if or when it comes.

How are you feeling? What are your plans? You sound so
very unperturbed, amidst all the screaming we hear from the
distant European shores.

He ended with some cheerless news about his books in
America: *'Goodbye to Berlin* is now the most utter flop, final and
irrevocable. Most people I meet don't even know it has been
published; even when they know my name and other writing quite
well. This is good for the soul, no doubt, but bad for the pocket.
My national debt is increasingly alarming.'
I found this a curious and illuminating failure of American
taste. *Goodbye to Berlin* had to wait for John Van Druten to turn
part of it into the play *I am a Camera* before it sailed into everyone's
consciousness. And this was not till 1951, when Dodie and Alec
Beesley (by design) dared him one afternoon to tackle it.
When Christopher and 'Vernon' reached Hollywood, they

settled in at first at 7136 Sycamore Trail, and had very soon made contact with Gerald Heard, Christopher Wood, and the Huxleys; and had made the acquaintance of Berthold Viertel's wife, Salka, script-writer to Greta Garbo and a power in the film world. He wrote to me in July:

Here I am living very quietly, seeing hardly anyone, and hoping vaguely that when Berthold arrives he will get me a movie job. Life with 'Vernon' reminds me very much of life with Heinz – except that he is even more serious, hates going out in the evenings, reads Suetonius, Wells and Freud, and goes to Art School. If I were happier inside myself I would be very happy. But I never cease worrying about Europe. My 'change of heart' about War, and the use of force generally, has only strengthened and been confirmed. I am sure this is how I will feel for the rest of my life. I'm afraid this will mean I shall lose a lot of friends but, I hope, none of the real ones. I am often very homesick for London, and the Hogarth Press office, Stephen's jokes about his psycho-analysis, walks with Morgan* near Abinger Hammer, Peggy's imitations, rows with my Mother. When I think of my friends, I remember them all laughing. The Past appears entirely in terms of jokes. The driving forces, which separate people, are so dull, really. Just their needs and greeds: sex and money and ambition. Oh dear, why do we have to have bodies? By the time they've been satisfied, there is only half an hour a day left over for Talk. And talk is all that finally matters.

He described the mood he was in more fully in this letter, and rather alarmed me.

Right now, I am like the ground under this part of California. I am settling down, and there is a 'fault' inside me which may produce earthquakes. So it is better to keep off me altogether. I am only too liable, literally, to let you down. For the last six weeks or more, I have been working on something for the autumn number of *New Writing*. First it was a piece

* E.M. Forster.

about New York; then it was a study of Toller.* Today I realized that neither of them will do. New York needs endless polishing. The Toller piece just sounds stupid and patronising and rather offensive. It has a certain smart-alecky value, but I was fond of Toller, and can't publish it as it stands. I doubt if you'd want to print it, either. So once again, I am the criminal, the oath-breaker. And, once again, I can only say I'm sorry.

John, I am so utterly sick of being a person – Christopher Isherwood, or Isherwood, or even Chris. Aren't you too? Don't you feel, more and more, that all your achievements, all your sexual triumphs, are just like cheques, which represent money, but have no real value? Aren't you sick to death of your face in the glass, and your business-voice, and your love-voice, and your signature on documents? I know I am.

He ended his letter with a confession that was news to me, though I had guessed that something of the sort was going on: 'As you may have gathered from the above remarks, I have become very much interested in Yoga philosophy, due to Gerald Heard. He is a very great man. A kind of walking Athens. And terribly funny. We see him a lot. Oh yes, and I met Huxley, who is nice, but oh so bookish and inclined to be pontifical . . . . Must go now and make the beds.'

Like many other friends of Christopher, I felt dismay at these hints of him becoming a convert to Yoga. Not only did I feel that it would draw him away from me, but I thought of Heard as rather a phoney. However, as Christopher's involvement grew deeper, I decided that I could not judge sensibly from London, and I never discussed the subject with him in letters, though frequently with his other English friends, who almost without exception expressed their anxiety and mystification. The conversion did, I think, create a gulf between him and Wystan who, ever more firmly holding to his family Anglicanism expressed the view that Yoga was 'mumbo-

* Isherwood's memoir of the poet Ernst Toller, 'The Head of a Leader', was published in the first issue of *Encounter* in 1953.

jumbo' and was not to be moved; it was not only that Wystan's life in New York grew to have less in common with Christopher's in the movie-world of California, though that was important in their gradual estrangement. I am pretty certain that Wystan would not have been sympathetic to Christopher's view of the ultimate necessity of writing about sainthood, as expressed in his 'Problems of the Religious Novel' in *Vedanta and the West*, any more than I was. Wystan was, I believe, never a pacifist in the sense that Christopher became one, when he faced up to the possibility that in a war he might have to fire at Heinz. The further stage of his argument that he couldn't shoot anyone in an opposing army because he might be somebody's Heinz seemed to me rather thin. After all, the number of those who have friends on both sides in a war must be rather small – though I was one of them myself. This condition caused me much agony of mind when I thought of my Austrian friends, but the need to defeat Hitler seemed to me over-riding. Though my war service was confined to the Home Guard, I could never have been the kind of all-out pacifist that Christopher had become, but I respected him for his decision if not for his logic.

And then the long-dreaded war broke out, and soon after the outbreak the persecution of Christopher and Wystan as deserters and cowards. Personally, I was very sorry that they were not going to be in England with us, not to know how they would have reacted to what we were about to experience, as we had the wonderful poems of Louis MacNeice (who came back from America) about the Blitz. There was an obstinate core of die-hards who seemed to have got it into their heads that the more vocal anti-fascists were *responsible* for the war. One thing that these head-hunters had forgotten, or chose deliberately to forget, was that Christopher and Wystan had left England at a time when war seemed to be indefinitely postponed in the comforting aftermath of the Munich agreement. In any case these critics had always disliked and suspected them, and now seemed a capital opportunity to strike. In the House of Commons Major Sir Jocelyn Lucas set the ball rolling by asking the Parliamentary Secretary to the Minister of Labour whether steps had been taken, or would be taken, to summon British citizens of military age, such as Mr W.H. Auden and Mr Christopher Isherwood, for registration and calling-up in view of the fact they were seeking refuge abroad. The popular press was soon in full cry, but the Government decided to do nothing, even if they had been able to do anything. What was particularly wounding for the two of them was that a snide attack was made on them from a side that should have been more sympathetic – in Cyril Connolly's new monthly, *Horizon*. I thought that this attack was contemptible myself, and much later, in 1942, it was followed by a satiric portrait of them in Evelyn Waugh's new novel *Put Out More Flags* as Parsnip and Pimpernel, 'two great poets who had recently fled to New York'. This was vicious, especially as Waugh was known to have admired Christopher's work, and it was distressing to see him joining the mob. I remember being much saddened by the hullabaloo, which struck me as grotesquely ill-informed and unfair, but that did not prevent me being irritated by the bland above-the-battle tone of Wystan's lines in *September 1st 1939*:

> There is no such thing as the State
> And no one exists alone;
> Hunger allows no choice
> To the citizen or the police;
> We must love one another or die . . . .

Christopher's case was not improved by a leak to the press of an indiscreet letter he had written to Gerald Hamilton about the ridiculous behaviour of some of the German refugees who were crowding into California. In this letter he said: 'I have no intention of coming back to England . . . .' This statement was in conflict with what he said, in various letters to various correspondents – that he would honour his pre-war commitment to the Foreign Office to work for them if required, or join the Red Cross or a Quaker ambulance unit, but in any case the situation was radically altered for him by America's entry into the war after Pearl Harbor, and the fact that he came thereafter under American draft law. He was by that time deep into Vedanta, had been initiated by Swami Prabhavananda and had asked him to be his guru. Very little about this crucially important development in his life came through in his letters to his friends

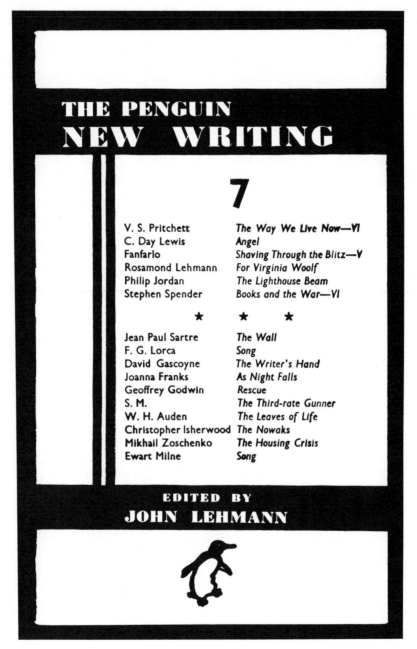

The front cover of the June 1941 edition of *Penguin New Writing*. The issue contained a reprint of Isherwood's 'The Nowaks', described by John Lehmann in his foreword as 'perhaps the finest story we have ever published'.

in England, though he wrote an account of his life at La Verne, where he had joined a seminar run by Gerald Heard in July 1941, which I printed in *Penguin New Writing* – by then established on its dizzily successful course. He still felt guilty about having written for me neither his promised piece on New York nor on Ernst Toller. He wrote to me on 3 July 1941: 'I feel so terribly sorry about all the times I've let you down that I rack my brains to find any conceivable way of appeasing you.' What he had an equally bad conscience about was having left in the lurch the English boy whom he had once so recklessly promised to take to New York. He kept on referring to this in his letters, and told me that he had finally plucked up courage to confess to the boy that he knew it wouldn't work and that he must abandon hope of joining him in the USA. But he instructed me by letter and cable to channel some of the royalties he was earning from his by now brilliantly successful *Goodbye to Berlin* to this boy, to help him pay for the courses he had undertaken at Christopher's suggestion.

Early on in the war he asked me to find and send him some books which he had left at his home in London. I therefore arranged a day with his mother when she would be coming up from the country, and went along to Pembroke Gardens. It was a most saddening experience to go into his room and see it all covered in dust sheets: it was as if he were dead, and all our years of collaboration finally extinguished. I was haunted by the abandoned look of that room for a long time, indeed until Christopher returned to England after the war. It was in the back of my mind every time I wrote to him. 'A Day at La Verne', when it came, seemed like a voice from a spirit world:

On the evening of July 7th, 1941, eighteen men and seven women met at one of the buildings of La Verne College, Southern California. Their intellectual, social and professional backgrounds differed widely. Perhaps they had nothing in common but a need, a need for a refreshed faith, a new kind of integration which would help them with the problem of their own muddled lives and the desperately anarchic world in which they lived. One should not imagine them as dedicated, or even specially devout. Some were frankly sceptical. Others winced at the sound of holy words which had been used to blackmail their childhood. A few were jealously on guard over the corpse of a dogma. Nearly all, at one time or another, had had a faint glimpse of some central Reality within themselves – a glimpse toward which they had feebly struggled for a while and then weakened, ruefully confessing their lack of condition. It was discipline and training which they hoped for here. We had gathered, as research-workers in any field may gather, to compare notes, to discuss techniques, and to get the inspiration which a feeling of companionship in effort can give . . . .

Next morning, our communal life began, according to the prearranged schedule. We were called at five o'clock. At five-thirty we gathered for an hour of group meditation. At seven, we had breakfast – in silence, while one of us read aloud. At nine, we met for an hour and a half of discussion. At eleven-thirty the midday meditation began. At one, we lunched and talked. Theoretically, the early part of the afternoon was free, but a few of us often met, in smaller units, to discuss some topic of general interest. At four there was another general discussion. At six, the evening meditation. At seven-thirty supper, with reading. At nine, bed . . . .

Looked at from the outside, such a programme of living as has been described above may appear unnatural, unhealthy and altogether fantastic. It did not seem so to those who took part in it . . . .

Fantastic it did indeed seem to his friends in London under the bombs, and fantastic in the life of the Christopher they had known. Some months before he had written to me:

I am just stuck in one of my sterile periods. So I confine myself to keeping a very detailed diary of my life here, which will provide me with plenty of raw material for later. It certainly is a very extraordinary life – one third German Refugee, one third Yoga and one third Metro-Goldwyn-Mayer, which has just given me a job, writing dialogue for a James Hilton story! I cannot say that I am happy, or ever could be, as long as this war lasts, but I am certainly going through one of the most interesting periods of my life, and learning a great deal. I see Berthold a lot. Huxley and Heard quite often. And

there are exotic glimpses of Garbo, Krishnamurti, Bertrand
Russell and Charlie Chaplin. I haven't yet met Mickey
Rooney, although I am now employed under the same roof, but
no doubt I shall.

The German Refugee part of his life was mainly in Salka Viertel's
circle, where the Manns and many other Germans in California
gathered. What he didn't say in this letter was that he had talked
the Vedanta people into accepting his homosexual life, the idea
being that any deep attachment to another human being was to
be deplored in a Yoga initiate, but the sex didn't matter. To his
English friends it looked as if he had found a way of having his
cake and eating it.

The MGM part of his life must eventually have been a
disappointment to him. He was kept very busily at work, partly
for MGM and partly for other film moguls, but very few of the
scripts he worked on were ever used for films – sometimes his
scripts were scratched and other script-writers were brought in,
sometimes they never got to shooting at all, sometimes he never
even got a credit when it was shot. He must have had a special
skill or he would not have got so many jobs. He was remarkably
cool and philosophical about it, and treated it all as a way of
making money while learning about the film-world. 'The studio,'
he said to a friend on one occasion, 'is just an office I visit in
the daytime.' The first serious opportunity he had was given him
by Gottfried, Max Reinhardt's son, an MGM producer who was
a friend of the Viertels, to write the dialogue for a screenplay
of James Hilton's *Rage in Heaven*, but though the film was made
it was ruined by squabbles on the set and was badly received.
In spite of this ill-omened start, he had been offered a year's
contract by MGM. He wrote to me in April 1940:

This studio has just finished *The Mortal Storm* – which will
probably be good, but terribly funny, because the nice Germans
are played by Americans, and the nasty ones by German
refugees. I am just about to start a picture about Chopin, who
is to be whitewashed for Robert Donat. Actually, I think he
was the most unpleasant of all geniuses. George Sand was much
too good for him . . . . First line of our picture: 'Hullo'. Last

line: 'Let's hope and pray he is.' You can guess the rest.

The picture was never made, but the work was obviously profitable for him, because he wrote: 'the weather is terrific – 94 in the shade – and all the beaches crowded. Money swirls around me like autumn leaves. I pick some of it and throw it away again – there is really nothing to spend it on; except the books which remind me of England. I have quite a library. All the poets.'

IX

In the same letter (16 April 1940) he gave vent to the feeling that had for long oppressed him, that his new-found pacifism was alienating him from the friends he had left in England:

Of course, the news from Europe makes one feel unspeakably wretched – especially as many people here regard it as an exciting football game, in which they would rather like to play. It is strange to live amongst these psychically virgin Californians, with their sound teeth and intact nerves. Partly it is very stimulating; partly it makes you feel lonely. Sometimes I think that I must return to Europe, anyhow, at any price – just to merge my invidual aches in the big general ache. I'm afraid I should feel myself just as much of an outcast there. There are few people I could honestly agree with, about this war. You would understand, I think. But what about Stephen, and the others? Believing what I do, there's simply no place for me in existing society – even in the opposition. And, not being a prophet, like Wystan, I can't raise my voice in the wilderness. The way things look now I shall most likely end up in prison – or, if I'm lucky, the Red Cross.

A year later, he wrote:

It's no use – I shall never write anything till this war's over. My voice is changing, like a choirboy's, and I can't find the new notes. But I am more certain than ever that something is happening inside (surely it is to everyone who isn't a stone, these days) and there will be something to show for this exile. Or perhaps I shouldn't call it exile – for I love California. If a dozen people I know were here, I couldn't imagine a better home. You must certainly join us, one day.

In the same letter he repeated, briefly, what he had told me in several previous letters: 'I am trying to get on, as hard as I can, with Yoga. It's what I think about most, nowadays.'

My knowledge at first hand of the early stages of Christopher's conversion to Yoga (though I dearly would have loved to talk it all over with him), up to the episode of La Verne, is gleaned entirely from such occasional remarks in his letters as I have just quoted. Nevertheless, in view of the fact that it became more and more important to him, I think I must try and insert a few notes of elucidation, derived from various statements at various times by Christopher himself (not in letters to me), and other sources. I do it without any firm conviction that I have got it right, never having been at any time in my life attracted to Yoga, and inclining rather to Auden's view that there is a lot of mumbo-jumbo in it, in spite of the fact that a dear and intelligent friend such as Christopher became a convert.

Christopher went out to California partly to get into the movie-world, but also to find re-affirmation and explanation from Gerald Heard of his newly found pacifism. But Gerald Heard was already practising Yoga in the sense that he had already acquired the habit of meditation and prayer as a means of coming closer to the Godlike Reality which is within every individual. He initiated Christopher into meditation and lectured him on the central meaning and aspirations of Vedanta, which is built on the ancient Hindu scriptures or Vedas. Christopher, having long ago discarded the traditional Christianity in which he had been brought up, and suffering from the profound spiritual confusion he described so vividly in his letters to me, was powerfully attracted by what Heard preached to him. Not long after he started his meditations and his study of Vedanta, he asked Heard to introduce him to Prabhavananda, the Swami who directed the Vedanta Society of Southern California. Prabhavananda was a very remarkable man, boyish-looking we are told though already in his forties, completely unaffected and unpretentious, with a remarkable gift for expounding Vedanta for the novices who were serious in their wish to learn. Christopher fell almost at once for his charm and simplicity, and some time that summer (1940) asked him to be his guru, or mentor, and initiate him into the mysteries of Vedanta with the ultimate idea of becoming a monk. The Vedanta Society had its home at 1946 Ivar Avenue, with an only recently erected temple in the garden. Heard already did his meditations twice a day for three hours each, but the Swami (a name which is roughly equivalent to 'Father' in Catholic parlance) counselled Christopher to start with something far less strenuous while he was learning. Christopher also made a clean breast of his need to work in the movie-world, and of his homosexuality, as I have already mentioned.

Christopher remained devoted to the Swami, as he describes in *My Guru and his Disciple* (published in England in 1980), and always received sympathy and ease of spirit from him even in the times when he felt he could no longer bear the discipline and rituals of becoming a Hindu monk – which he never did become – or when the old life of sexual promiscuity beckoned with a fatal attraction. His devotion was strongly reinforced by a task they undertook together, of translating the Hindu epic, the *Bhagavad-Gita*, which itself is part of a greater epic, the *Mahabharata*. The Swami prepared a rough translation into English from the Sanskrit, and Christopher's task was to turn it into a polished style that would be acceptable to English readers. After they had been at work on it for some months they put the result of their labours before an intelligent English friend, Margaret Kiskadden. Her judgement was discouraging. She felt that there was too much un-English locution, archaic and clumsy, too much too close to the original Sanskrit, and that the general effect was as awkward as that of earlier English versions. Christopher had let Aldous Huxley see it, and he had agreed with her. The two translators had at first been profoundly depressed by this verdict. Then suddenly Christopher had a flash of inspiration, and translated the opening passages into verse with a strong rhythmic beat. Encouraged by the effect this had on the Swami and their adviser, he set about re-casting the whole version into a mixture of verse and prose, which he believed would more effectively render the quality of the original. This was the version which was eventually published, and gave them confidence to tackle various other translations from the Sanskrit. At the same time it seems to have loosened the writing block that Christopher had been suffering from. He had started a new short novel rather earlier, but had put it aside. This he now took up again, as he described in his letter to me of 9 January 1943:

before the sudden call to the movie-swamp stopped it, I was beginning a study of Berthold working at Gaumont British, which I intend to call *Prater Violet*. And, after that, I want to do the story of Heinz. And, after that, a somewhat modified version of 'Paul is Alone' (remember ?). Three novelettes, to make a volume. Is it just a dream? I don't know. I was as excited as hell when I got ready to start: the only trouble is that I'll have to find a new *tone of voice*: because the ventriloquist has changed somehow, and needs a new dummy . . .

Eventually the short novel was published by itself, in America in 1945 and in England the following year, as *Prater Violet*. Christopher was always planning combinations and permutations of his shorter novels, and in this case the material of 'Paul is Alone' was transformed into the last episode of *Down There on a Visit*, while 'the story of Heinz' never got written at all, for though Waldemar lived with the narrator on the Greek island in 'Ambrose', he can only be considered a shadow of Heinz. *Prater Violet* showed that the old magician had lost none of his cunning: the structure was masterly, the pace beautifully controlled, and Dr Bergmann one of his most brilliant tragi-comic creations. The 'tone of voice' which had worried Christopher so much was largely settled by the fact that Dr Bergmann was a German refugee and that much of the dialogue was in movie-jargon; but the new

Christopher made himself heard in the last scene where an almost mystical relationship, of spiritual father and son, is hinted at between Bergmann and the narrator.

In the same letter Christopher, who had just seen the Penguin with 'A Day at La Verne' in it, wrote:

I was very embarrassed by my La Verne thing; it reads like the parish magazine; but I'm sure you did right to print it. It administers a kind of sour sip of quinine flavored with prigdom. I wouldn't feel I had to do so much apologizing, now; or be so gloomy. I sound as if I were being exiled to the salt mines, instead of starting a new life of the most absorbing interest and adventure, which this has actually been and is being . . . . They recently lowered the age-limit, so I'm going to live at the Vedanta 'monastery' here in Hollywood, as from next month: more about this in another letter . . . . Well, I must stop for now, with so much love as ever, and God bless you, John, in 1943. You're one of my last real links with England, now. But we'll meet again, and before long, I feel.

Christopher's euphoria about living at the 'monastery' does not seem to have lasted very long. The chief trouble, one cannot help feeling, was sexual restlessness. I do not know what caused 'Vernon' to go back to New York at the end of 1941, but in any case it was not the end of their relationship. They continued to correspond at long intervals, and then in the end he came back to California, because it seemed Christopher needed him. Meanwhile Christopher had various affairs, one particularly intense one with a beautiful young man he calls Alfred, which faded out as soon as 'Vernon' reappeared at the end of August. It is possible that Christopher's new friendship with Tennessee Williams, insatiably promiscuous, had something to do with his increasing restlessness. There was also the influence of another new friendship, which became increasingly important in Christopher's life at this time. Denny Fouts was born in Florida, and when he was sixteen was swept off from home by a passing cosmetics tycoon to begin his career as the Best Kept Boy in the World. His sexual successes included a large variety of rich and aristocratic connections of both sexes, and just before the war he landed up in the household in Paris of Peter Watson, heir to a margarine fortune, who was to finance Cyril Connolly's *Horizon*, when he moved to London very soon after. In 1940, when the German attacks on London intensified, Peter insisted on him going back to the USA.

I am uncertain when exactly Denny Fouts met Christopher, but according to *Down There on a Visit* 'Paul' met him in the autumn of 1940 at a Californian restaurant in the company of Connolly's American wife who had come back to the USA with Denny. Christopher was very much intrigued with this already legendary male prostitute, and struck up a friendship with him – though it does not appear to have been sexual. Denny or 'Paul' showed an interest in Heard ('Augustus Parr') and persuaded Christopher to introduce them. Christopher never said much about Denny in his letters to me, probably because he was aware that I had met him in Paris just before the war, and had not taken to him. But we know from *My Guru and his Disciple* that Denny wanted to try the Yogi life of meditation and ritual, though a meeting between him and the Swami had been a disaster, and when Christopher moved into a new apartment in March 1941 he invited Denny to share it with him and join with him in an experiment of strict Yogi observances as if they were training to be 'monks'. This lasted very well until in August Denny, who as a conscientious objector had been assigned for service in a forestry camp, got his summons and had to leave. The La Verne seminar had started by then.

After La Verne, Christopher spent some time with the Quakers, who had set up a programme at Haverford, just outside Philadelphia, the aim of which was to help German-speaking refugees to learn about the American way of life and way of teaching. Christopher seems to have found the experience bracing and satisfying, and plunged into all the activities, not only tutoring the inmates but also doing the physical work and household chores. He also made an especial friend of a young lecturer in Spanish, by the name of Réné Blanc-Roos, who was already a warm if critical admirer of his work. Christopher believed that Blanc-Roos had helped him to overcome his writing block, and dedicated *Prater Violet* to him. The hostel closed in July 1942, by which time Pearl Harbor had taken place and America had entered the war. As Christopher had taken out his first papers to become an American subject, he was liable to the draft. He had no difficulty in being registered for non-combatant duties, but as the age limit for the draft was lowered soon after, he was never in fact called up.

In the period directly after La Verne and Haverford, he entered what he called the 'movie-swamp' again, though he had no more luck than before in furthering his ill-starred career as a script-writer. He began work on a Somerset Maugham story, *The Hour Before Dawn*, in which his main contribution was to give plausibility to a tribunal scene for conscientious objectors; but the film was never made. After that he did some work on a film version of Wilkie Collins's *The Woman in White*, but nearly all his contribution had vanished in the screen version eventually used. He then worked on a script with Aldous Huxley about a faith-healer, to be called *Jacob's Hands*, but none of the studios would touch it. They were amazed afterwards to discover that this was because the studios were afraid of alienating the medical establishment. Christopher was working with Warner Brothers during most of 1945, but again nothing reached the screen. During this time he frequently mixed with the stars of the movie world, Greta Garbo and Charlie Chaplin and his wife Oona, whom he met through Salka Viertel's salon. Meanwhile 'Vernon' had come to California again, but the new relationship with Christopher did not last. However, during the latter half of 1945, a new personality entered his life and had considerable influence for some years. Bill Caskey was an outstanding photographer of much charm and wit, who had come from a background of Kentucky horse-people. His drawbacks were a violent temper and too great a fondness for hard liquor. Christopher was captivated and stimulated, and took him to live with him in an apartment over Salka Viertel's garage in Mabery Road. He took him to South America, as companion and photographer, on the six months' visit that produced *The Condor and the Cows*, in the winter of 1947-8.

Even well before the war was over, in writing to announce how his work was going, he showed how his thoughts were turning more and more towards his old friends in Europe and his old haunts.

The Gita translation is finished at last, and I believe not bad. I wonder what you will think of it. Now I can get to work on my own stuff, and really discover what it is I want to write. I have to pick up the knitting where I dropped it: but maybe it will be another kind of sock. Anyhow, never believe Tony (Bower)* or anyone else who says I have stopped writing. I know that I'll write to my dying day . . . . I seem to spend more and more of my time with you, and others who aren't here; and there is a curiously satisfactory feeling of communication. I refuse to believe that the difference in the kind of lives we have been leading is really important, and I believe that when we meet we shall pick up the threads much more easily than we suppose. We seem to have moved apart and together again . . . .

And again, a few months later: 'There are many people I often wonder about – dozens and dozens. I suppose they are all alive and intensely busy, somewhere. I suppose I shall even see some of them again one day, unbelievable as it seems. I shall certainly have to come to England for a while as soon as the war is over, to see my Mother, who is getting old, and make various arrangements. I dread the sadness of that visit . . . .'

* A friend of both Isherwood and Lehmann.

C hristopher fell rather ill for part of the winter of 1945-6, and was in hospital for an operation. He had planned his visit to England for the summer of 1946, but it had to be postponed. It was not till January 1947 that he finally took off from New York for London via Gander and Shannon. He has left a very vivid account of this visit in an article for my 'Coming to London' series in the *London Magazine*. He begins by describing the air journey, and then goes on:

throughout the years I had spent in Hollywood, I had never tired of protesting against the American film presentation of English life. What caricature! What gross exaggeration! But now – and increasingly during the weeks that followed – I began to reverse my judgement. *Is* it possible to exaggerate the Englishness of England? Even the bus which took us from the airport into London seemed grotesquely 'in character'; one almost suspected that it had been expressly designed to amaze foreign visitors. By nature a single-decker, it had had a kind of greenhouse grafted insecurely on to its back. Riding in this was much more alarming than flying. We whizzed down narrow lanes with barely room enough to pass a pram, scraping with our sides the notorious English hedgerows; then slowed with a jerk to circle a roundabout – an *Alice in Wonderland* death trap guaranteed to wreck any driver doing more than five miles an hour. And then we would pass through an English village complete with a village church in a country churchyard; so absurdly authentic that it might have been lifted bodily off a movie-lot at MGM . . . . And as for the accents that I now began to hear around me – I could scarcely trust my ears. Surely they were playing it *very* broad? Half the population appeared to be talking like Richard Haydn as a Cockney bank clerk, the other half like Basil Rathbone as Sherlock Holmes.

I saw little of London that night, for I went straight to John Lehmann's house*; and there a welcome awaited me that I shall never forget. Looking around me at the faces of my old friends, I discovered a happy paradox – namely that, while England seemed fascinatingly strange, my friends and our friendship seemed to be essentially what they had always been, despite the long separation. That was what was to make my visit so wonderful and memorable.

Christopher had written to me from Santa Monica in December that 'I'm a Yank now – but don't be alarmed – you'd never know it.' Perhaps he didn't realize that his accent and some of his mannerisms had changed so much. We noticed at once. These changes did not, however, show themselves continuously: I had the impression, talking to him during the three months of his visit, that he was, in spirit, being pulled to and fro across the Atlantic all the time. His article went on:

During my re-exploration of London, I got two strong impressions; of shabbiness and of goodwill. The Londoners themselves were shabby – many of them stared longingly at my new overcoat – and their faces were still wartime faces, lined and tired. But they didn't seem depressed or sullen. This may sound like a stupidly sweeping statement by a casual visitor, but I have seen a thoroughly depressed nation – the German in 1932. The English were not in the least like that.

* 31 Egerton Crescent, where Lehmann had moved to in 1945.

Christopher Isherwood photographed by Howard Coster in 1936,
'A cross between a cavalry major and a rather prim landlady'?

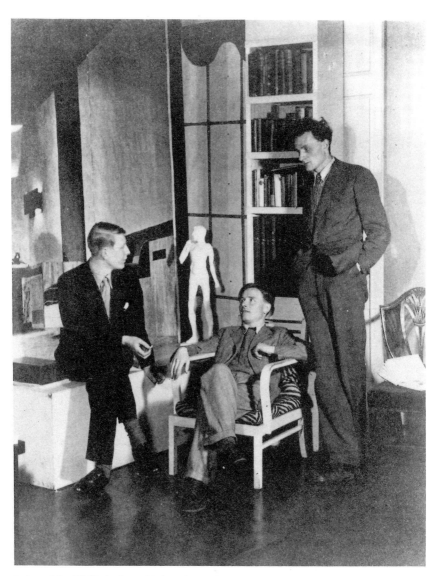

Left to right, W.H.Auden, Christopher Isherwood and Stephen Spender
in the thirties, close friends and 'out to create an entirely new literature'.

Christopher and Heinz in 1934, a picture taken in Tenerife
in the banana grove where most of *Mr Norris* was written.

Christopher Isherwood photographed by Benjamin Britten in the thirties.

Two scenes from the original Group Theatre production of Isherwood and Auden's *The Dog Beneath the Skin* at the Westminster Theatre in 1936. *Above*, 'Have you seen Sir Francis Crewe? *Below*, Mad masks in the red-light district of Ostnia.

There was a great deal of publicity about Isherwood and Auden's departure for China on 19 January 1938, with cameras at Victoria - all thoroughly enjoyed by Christopher.

Christopher Isherwood and W.H.Auden in Central Park, July 1938, during their 'nine days' wonder' visit to New York.

John Lehmann photographed in 1939, a 'tall handsome young personage with his pale narrowed quizzing eyes'.

Christopher Isherwood, E.M.Forster and William Plomer at Aldeburgh in June 1948, photographed by Bill Caskey.

A snapshot of Christopher taken in the early fifties. 'His expression was
remarkably boyish, and remained so . . . There was a twinkle in his eye which
he seemed to be able to switch on and off like an actor.'

John Lehmann with his two sisters, Beatrix, the actress,
and Rosamond the novelist, photographed in August 1953.

Christopher Isherwood
photographed in London, May 1965.

John Lehmann in 1980. 'Seated behind his desk, John seemed the incarnation
of authority – benevolent authority, but authority, none the less.'

Christopher and Don Bachardy in June 1972.

A lithograph of Christopher and Don Bachardy done in 1976 by David Hockney.

For instance, the girls at the ration board, which surely must have been the most exasperating of jobs, were quite gratuitously pleasant. 'It seems so silly', one of them remarked to me, 'to have to call Americans *aliens*.' And this wasn't just a chance encounter with a solitary xenophile, for I heard another girl being extremely sympathetic to a native lady with an obviously unreasonable grievance. On another occasion, when I was on a train, a young couple sat next to me who were about to emigrate to Australia; their baggage, already labelled for the voyage, proclaimed this fact. The other passengers in my compartment congratulated the couple on their decision and questioned them eagerly about their plans – all this without the slightest hint of bitterness or criticism. Of course this goodwill was somewhat of the grin-and-bear-it variety, but it had cer-tainly made London a much friendlier place to visit. The only negative aspect of it was, perhaps, that the English had become a little too docile in their attitude towards official regulations. 'We're a nation of queue-formers,' someone said . . . . London's shabbiness was another matter; it didn't seem to me to have a cheerful side. The actual bomb damage gave you a series of sudden shocks – as when, one evening, I spent some time ringing the doorbell of a house, until I happened to look up through the fanlight and saw that the place was an empty shell, smashed wide open to the stars. Yet the shabbiness was more powerfully and continuously depressing. Plaster was peeling from even the most fashionable squares and crescents; hardly a building was freshly painted. In the Reform Club, the wallpaper was hanging down in tatters. The walls of the National Gallery showed big unfaded rectangles, where pictures had been removed and not yet rehung. Many once stylish restaurants were now reduced to drabness and even squalor. The shortage of materials made all but the most urgent repairs illegal . . . . London's shabbiness was so sad, I thought, because it was unwilling – quite unlike the cheerful down-at-heel air of some minor Latin American capital. London remembered the past and was ashamed of its present appearance.

Christopher was excited, during those two days he spent with me, a little confused by the war-time changes he had already noticed, and a little nervous about the way he would be received.

We soon, I think, put him at his ease – as many of his old friends as could be mustered to meet him in person, and others who were on the telephone as soon as the news got round. None of us had joined the scapegoat chase in which politicians and journalists who had never known them (or most likely their works) had tried to vilify him and Auden as 'escapers'. We had been sorry not to have him during the weird, sometimes apocalyptic and frightening experiences we had been through; we had been a little sceptical, while the bombs were falling, of his mystical exercises in Yoga temples and monasteries; we were immensely glad to have him back, even for so short a time as he planned to stay with us, even in this slightly transmogrified form. We noted that the face, deeply tanned by the Californian sun, was a little more lined; but that the deep-set eyes, though opened wide in respectful amazement or horror at the tales we had to tell, twinkled with the same old impish appreciation of anything comical or fantastic. We noted that his favourite talk was of Hollywood and movie-stars; and we wondered sometimes whether he didn't in fact see us as characters in a film – an American film of little old England heroically carrying on in spite of all trials and tribulations.

After these all too brief days of happy reunion with his old friends and getting the feel of post-war London, Christopher went straight up North to see his mother and his brother Richard at the old family home of Wyberslegh Hall in Cheshire, which he found in a thoroughly run-down condition. 'I was never meant for these latitudes,' he cried in his first letter to me, 'and I huddle miserably in front of a blue gas-fire. London seems almost as remote as America. If only we lived there still! I spend most of the time reading my old diaries (goodness what energy I had in those days! It's a marvel I'm not impotent) and washing dishes. My mother hasn't changed a bit. She does all the cooking. But Nanny is very, very old . . . .' And in the next: 'Being up here is like a steamship journey. You just screw down the porthole and weather it out. I have all my letters, photographs and books to amuse me. Turning over the pages of *Evil Was Abroad* I wished so much you'd write another novel. Will you? Please . . . .' Later on he went down to Cheltenham to stay with his old friends Olive Mangeot and Jean Ross. He tried to get over to Stratford to see Beatrix who was playing an assortment of parts, including Viola, Portia, Isabella and the Nurse in *Romeo and Juliet*, but swirling floods cut them off from one another.

In his article for the 'Coming to London' series he tried to give an outsider's impression of the rigours of that terrible winter:

Few of my readers will need to be reminded that this was the winter of the coal shortage and the great blizzards. The snow started a week after my arrival; and it soon assumed the aspect of an invading enemy. Soldiers turned out to fight it with flamethrowers. The newspapers spoke of it in quasi-military language: 'Scotland isolated', 'England cut in half'. Even portions of London were captured; there was a night when no taxi driver would take you north of Regent's Park. With coal strictly rationed, gas reduced to a blue ghost and electricity often cut off altogether, everybody in London was shivering. I remembered how the actors played to nearly empty houses, heroically stripped down to their indoor clothes, while we their audience huddled together in a tight clump, muffled to the chins in overcoats, sweaters and scarves. I remember a chic lunch party composed of the intellectual *beau monde*, at which an animated discussion of existentialism was interrupted by one of the guests exclaiming piteously 'Oh, I'm so *cold*!' Two or three of my friends said to me then: 'Believe us, this is worse than the war!' By which I understood them to mean that the situation couldn't by any stretch of the imagination be viewed as a challenge to self-sacrifice or an inspiration to patriotism; it was merely hell.

Nevertheless, I have to confess, with the egotism of a tourist, that the blizzard did a great deal to 'make' my visit. It gave me a glimpse of the country in crisis which helped me to some faint idea of what the war years had been like. And, besides this, the cold certainly increased one's energy and sharpened one's senses. There was a great deal to be seen in London that winter – particularly in the art galleries, where many new and talented painters were exhibiting. It was then that I acquired, though only to a very modest degree, the good habit of buying pictures.

Before he went back to America on the *Queen Elizabeth*, he returned to London for a few days of parties and leave-takings. This gave me the opportunity to introduce him to some of the younger artists I had been featuring in *Penguin New Writing*, in particular Keith Vaughan, to whose work he had taken a special liking; he in fact bought several paintings of Vaughan's to take back with him to America. He also promised to do all he could on that side of the Atlantic for my new publishing firm, which I had started the year before when the break with Leonard Woolf occurred. He wrote to me on arrival in New York:

Just to tell you that I arrived on Friday, after a bugger of a voyage, with strong head-gales. I avoided being sick by doggedly overeating and dosing myself with whisky. We were all vaccinated, which made me a bit sick after landing but I'm fine now. Jimmy (Stern)'s* apartment is a dream (I even have a room all to myself to work in) and Caskey is sweeter than ever, and I am very very happy. I even think I'll like New York this time, anyhow till it gets really hot. So far, I've only seen Wystan, who was eager for all the London news.

My trip to England was wonderful, largely thanks to you. I can't ever tell you how much your kindness helped me through the first dubious moments and made me feel welcome. I only hope I wasn't a dreadful nuisance. Caskey was delighted with the Keith Vaughans, and they will occupy key positions in our living-room and be viewed by thousands. We'll try to do our part in building up his American reputation.

In a few days I hope to start driving the plough over the terrain for my new novel. I have terrible stage-fright about it but the only thing is to make a start. At all costs, I'm resolved, this time, not to be funny. I don't care how dreary and boring it is, as long as it isn't the kind of book anybody could possibly read for pleasure on a train. People resent being amused more than anything, I've decided.

This was, I thought, a curious statement from the creator of Mr Norris and Sally Bowles; but it is true that *The World*

---

* An Irish writer, published in *New Writing*, who lived in New York at this time.

in the Evening didn't turn out a very funny book. And Christopher's hope of enjoying New York life at last was quite soon dashed.

XI

Christopher's plan to devote the next few months to preparing the ground for his new novel was postponed by a fresh project. He had been offered a contract to write a travel book by both Methuen in London and Random House in New York, and he and Bill Caskey set out for their six months' wandering in South America on 19 September 1947. He must have written to me a number of letters from various points of stay, but they have mysteriously all disappeared, except for a few postcards. In Buenos Aires he met the famous editor of the literary magazine *Sur*, Victoria Ocampo, who had already been in correspondence with *New Writing* for several years; and also, to his surprise, the original 'German Boy' of his first adventures in Berlin, Berthold or Bubi, as he then called him. Bubi, now prosperous after many setbacks, was delighted to see Christopher, and proudly showed him a row of his books on the shelves of his living-room – though he couldn't yet read English.

On their way back they spent several days in Paris, where they chanced to meet Wystan and Chester on their way to Ischia, and made a new friend: Gore Vidal, who was a tremendous admirer of Christopher, and who knew that he had thought very highly of his homosexual novel, *The City and the Pillar* (which I had published in England, not without difficulty). They remained very good friends to the end, and Christopher dedicated *A Single Man* to him. They also paid a sad, farewell visit to Denny Fouts, who was seriously ill from drug excesses in Peter Watson's flat. He died the following year in Rome.

Christopher and Bill spent the latter part of June and early July 1948 in London, and while they were there a new offer of film work arrived from MGM. The job was to revise a script based on Dostoevsky's *The Gambler* which had already been worked on by Ladislas Fodor. Christopher found the work difficult, as his own ideas did not blend easily with Fodor's. He wrote to me from his new address in Santa Monica, 333 East Rustic Road, on 6 November:

My life, since I reached California, has been divided into two phases. The first, before Caskey joined me, was work at the studio, on the Dostoevsky picture, which is now being shot. (Called *The Great Sinner* – did you know he actually meditated writing a book of that name, the old ham!?) It is not Dostoevsky, but it is somewhat magnificent, owing to $3,000,000 worth of sets, costumes and highpowered talent. Anyhow, I disclaim all responsibility – unless, of course, you like it! This first phase also included a lot of whisky drinking and a good deal of running around town, in the process of which I lost nearly ten pounds and a great deal of sleep. Then Caskey arrived and found this house, which we hope to stay in for a couple of years. It is very nice, and really quite rustic, under some sycamores, near the ocean, beside a creek. I feel like Vanzetti's description of Sacco 'a worker from his boyhood, with a good job and pay, a bank account, a good and lovely wife, and a neat little home at the verge of a wood, near a brook . . . .' Madly respectable!

Caskey paints, carpenters, sews and cooks untiringly, and so far we have had only *one* wild party. I am churning out a travel-book, which is going to be my longest and worst work, I fear. I just can't do straight journalism, and the truth is that South America *bored* me, and I am ashamed that it bored me, and I hate it for making me feel ashamed. However, I am determined to go through with it and then get on with the novel, which at least will be an *honourable* failure.

The Condor and the Cows, as the travel book was called when it was finished, proved to have many fans, particularly in England, where it was chosen *Evening Standard* 'Book of the Month' when it came out in 1949. It was illustrated with nearly a hundred photographs taken by Bill Caskey. Later on, Christopher revised his opinion of the book, and even came to regard it as one of his best. The work on it, and the Dostoevsky contract for MGM, and, it must be admitted, the whisky drinking, meant that the new novel progressed very slowly indeed, but go on it did.

The story of how *Sally Bowles* was turned into the play *I am a Camera* has often been told, but I cannot refrain from relating the circumstances again here, as they were told to me. It seems that about this time Christopher was beginning to be worried about his finances. The advances on the travel book had long been exhausted, and the money from MGM for the Dostoevsky script had just kept him going since then. His friends were worried for him, too, and in particular Dodie Smith and her husband Alec Beesley. It occurred to them that one of the best ways for him to earn some money would be for *Sally Bowles* to be dramatized, and that the ideal person to do the job would be John Van Druten, who had a ranch near Palm Springs, and who had already had some professional dealings with Christopher. Their plan was to put the idea into Van Druten's mind as a challenge and as if by chance one day. Van Druten swallowed the bait, and produced a draft play, assimilating other parts of *Goodbye to Berlin* into Sally's story, in a few weeks. He also found the money to back it, and though Christopher wasn't over-enthusiastic about it in script, it was put on in Hartford, Connecticut at the beginning of November 1951. Christopher told me frequently afterwards that he was quite sure that Julie Harris as Sally made it a success, giving a fantastically brilliant performance of creative imagination. It was transferred to the Empire Theatre in New York at the end of November, and in spite of the reservations of some of the critics it soon became clear that it was going to be a big hit. A British production, with Dorothy Tutin as Sally, was put on in 1954, and was also a hit. Christopher made money out of both these productions, and continued to make much needed money. It was the biggest break he had had since he came to the USA, and continued to have, with some money coming in for the rest of his life, especially when the play was followed by a film, and the film by a musical, and the musical by a film of the musical with Liza Minnelli in the star part.

Meanwhile, the work on the new novel went slowly forward, but with many doubts and problems. One of the chief problems was the tone of voice, which had been masked in *Prater Violet* by the fact that the main character was a foreigner who spoke in the narrative in rather broken English. He wrote to me in April 1951:

Am pleased to report that my novel is really moving. But much to do yet. It's the most complicated bitch of a thing I ever attempted. After this, I go back to old poker-face Christopher Isherwood and his reportage. Real novels are too difficult. We are as poor as mice and Bill is working as a gardener. But this house is delightful. I do wish I could come over, but don't dare to move until the rough draft of the novel is finished. And no money.

It was not till September 1952 that I was given a further report on the novel – and on his relationship with Bill Caskey:

Billy is in Japan, working on a boat which goes via Hong Kong, Manila, to Singapore – and then home. I'll see him in November. He is blissfully happy, and so is our relationship. I emphatically do *not* agree with Cocteau's '*mes soeurs, n'aimez pas les marins*! . . . The novel goes very slow, but steady. I'm sure I'll finish it now, but am not so sure it isn't a bit gooey. Love, love, love, love! All the characters are either female or queer.

And, finally, at the end of October 1953, when the *London Magazine* had just been founded,*

I think I would like to do you a Los Angeles letter . . . .

* Lehmann founded and edited the *London Magazine*.

Just as soon as some revisions are finished on my novel. The American publisher (Random House) is more critical of it than Alan White (Methuen) – ironically enough, more bothered by some censorship problems – but he seems to like it very much, too; and I can meet his objections without throwing out anything I honestly like. This job should take, let's say, three more weeks.

The World in the Evening had been sent to his publishers on both sides of the Atlantic in August, when he had confessed to Edward Upward that it was 'terribly slipshod, and vulgar and sentimental in a Hollywoodish way'. Personally I felt that there was something wrong with almost all the characters – they didn't ring true – particularly the protagonist, Stephen Monk, and the writing all through lacked the usual zest. Part of the trouble, I feel sure, lay in the fact that the author was dealing with heterosexual relationships beyond his normal range, while the homosexual relationship between Charles and Bob, even in the re-written version, gives an almost embarrassing impression of arch coyness at times. His increasing obsession with sainthood, foreshadowed in his article 'Problems of the Religious Novel', which had originally appeared in *Vedanta and the West*, is shown in the character of Aunt Sarah, and is not fully convincing. One original touch was his brief exposition of Low Camp and High Camp, which was to have considerable influence on his generation and indeed pass into the language, but this one prophetic and witty passage does not redeem the whole novel. I think that most of Christopher's admirers would agree with his own later judgement, that *The World in the Evening* was his 'worst novel'.

Meanwhile his anxiety about his finances was removed by an offer that came out of the blue in January 1954 from MGM for him to write a filmscript on the theme of Henri II of France, Diane de Poitiers and Catherine de Medici, which occupied him until September. This windfall was increased by the sale of the reprint rights in *The World in the Evening*, and a bumper cheque for the smash hit of *I am a Camera* in London. During the years that followed, he was much occupied with what he described in his letters as his Mexican novel, the idea for which came to him on a brief trip to Mexico he made in the winter of 1954-5.

This eventually formed the basis of *Down There on a Visit*, though much altered in scope and scene; in fact little remained of his original ideas except the title. He had also made several new friends, one of whom became of major importance to him: Igor Stravinsky. It took Christopher, not a very musical person at the best, some time to appreciate Stravinsky's compositions, but he was immediately attracted by the man's natural warmth. In an interview on one occasion, he observed:

> I always think of Stravinsky in a very physical way. He was physically adorable; he was so cuddly – he was so little, and you wanted to protect him. He was very demonstrative, a person who – I suppose it was his Russian-ness – was full of kisses and embraces. He had great warmth. He would be fearfully hostile and snub people and attack his critics and so forth, but personally, he was a person of immense joy and warmth.

He was also a frequent drinking companion of Christopher's, being especially fond of a drink he called Marc de Bourgogne, which was dangerously strong for Christopher's rather low level of alcoholic tolerance, while Stravinsky's own level seemed beyond reach.

In the early fifties he continued to see Bill Caskey in between his voyages, but in spite of the remarks I have quoted from his letter to me in September 1952, Bill's so frequent absences at sea undoubtedly put a strain on their relationship, especially for a person of Christopher's wayward sexual habits. At the end of their South American journey, after the visit to Paris, he had brought Bill to London with him, as was natural. Their stay at Egerton Crescent was a delight, short though it was, and gave me the only opportunity I ever had of seeing them together. On Christopher's third trip to England, at the end of 1951, Bill didn't or couldn't accompany him, but as the trip had as its main object Christopher's long-meditated but often postponed and rather dreaded visit to post-war ruined Berlin, which he obviously had to make alone, it was inevitable. It so happened that I had just started *New Soundings*, my 'magazine on the air', and Christopher arrived in London in time to take part in the second of the series.

He gave a highly characteristic performance in reading a script
on six up-and-coming young American writers: he chose Ray
Bradbury, Truman Capote, William Styron, Speed Lamkin,
Norman Mailer and Calder Willingham. He was very confidential
in manner, serious and yet managing to give the impression that
some of the information he was giving his audience was peculiarly
funny, so that he could hardly refrain from chuckling. I can still
hear the mischievous relish that gradually came into his voice
as he spoke about Capote and the Southern school of writers that
seemed at that moment to dominate the American literary scene:

> There are, in fact, two Souths that people write about.
> One is the real contemporary South, a land where industriali-
> zation is increasing, education is spreading and considerable
> progress is being made towards solving the Negro problem. The
> other is the gothic-romantic, macabre South of decaying
> mansions, degenerate families, despair, drink, Spanish moss,
> sexual atrocities and lynchings. Truman writes about this
> second kind of South, and makes it just as gothic, funny and
> macabre as he knows how. I must confess that this second kind
> of South bores me utterly – its cult can in some ways be
> compared with the cult of a romantic Ireland which flourished
> at the beginning of this century – and the greatest tribute I can
> pay to Capote's talent is to say that nevertheless I sincerely
> admire his two novels (this was before the publication of *In Cold
> Blood*) . . . . He can be very funny and very touching. But I
> can't help feeling that he is often guilty of playing with the
> reader, as if trying to see just how much weirdness he can get
> away with . . . .

This second programme ran into a crisis. The script was
ready, the performers all booked, when the news came through
of the death of King George VI. All scheduled broadcasting
programmes were immediately cancelled, even on the Third
Programme. Nevertheless we recorded it at exactly the same time
that evening as if it had been going out, and Christopher departed
for Berlin, with an assignment for the *Observer* to write two articles
about his impressions and reactions. He returned about a fortnight
later, very eager to hear all details about the King's funeral. He
was particularly entranced by the gush some of the newspapers

had indulged in, which I had kept for him; especially the *Times* reporter who wrote of a blackbird 'trilling its sweet requiem' in the silence of Hyde Park Corner as the procession passed by.

Christopher told us with some emotion of his reunion with Heinz, whom he found living in East Berlin, happily married and with only pleasant remembrance of the times he and Christopher had spent together wandering across Europe before the war. He also described his visit to his old landlady, Fräulein Thurau, whose shrieks of excitement could be heard throughout the block when he rang at her door, and how they danced together in the street. A day or two after his return he fell into one of his fits of despair, burnt all his unanswered letters, told the BBC he couldn't do a talk he had promised them and gave them their money back, and got out of the second article for the *Observer*. He felt beleaguered and embittered by the journalists.

Before he left for Berlin, I put on a party for him, only fifteen of us in all, to meet again some of the people he had got to know while staying with me, including Henry Green,* Walter Baxter, of whose *Look Down in Mercy*§ I had become a tremendous admirer, and some of the younger artists Christopher had grown specially interested in. The party had a relaxed, intimate atmosphere; but the best part of the evening was the dinner at the Brompton Grill Christopher and I had afterwards, tête-à-tête, when he talked of his emotional life and its relationship to his writings, and its difficulties, more frankly than I could remember him doing since the old days in Europe; and he urged me to talk of my life in the same way. It was a real opening of our hearts to one another. We had so much to tell one another that we continued it over a lunch a few days later: I thought how close we had become on this visit, with whatever tension had existed since the war wiped right away. I had just had a crucial interview with the Harveys, who now owned my firm, at Paulton, and he agreed entirely with the attitude I was determined to take. He said: 'In Hollywood one starts by saying Yes, but gets to the top by saying No.' He lent me the war-time journal he had kept

---

* The novelist.
§ *Look Down in Mercy* was Walter Baxter's first novel.

after reaching California: I couldn't but find it fascinating as it filled in the long blank in my knowledge of his life when Europe was fading in his mind; though as I read on, I found it more and more concerned with people I knew nothing of, except here and there the name of a film-star. But what astonished and even perplexed me about it was the sort of schizophrenia it revealed between the new Vedanta beliefs he was adopting and what seemed to me the entirely unrelated, unchanged, uncoordinated life of the old Christopher which went on at the same time. I was also struck by how terribly little he had recorded about his pre-occupations as a writer, as if he wanted to try and fulfil himself in every way except as a writer, as an artist.

I was able, before he left, to take him down to Sussex in the car, and show him the cottage I had acquired only a couple of years before, the garden not yet completely finished. He was enchanted, and, I thought, a little envious. Alexis* and I did much work potting bulbs and planting primulas while he dozed by the fire. In the car he confessed to me that his friends in England had become a sort of mythology for him, so that even if they died while he was away in America, they would still be there for him, talking in his mind. And he repeated how unforgettable an event his first landing in England in 1947 had been for him.

Last farewells were said to Christopher in the library at No.31 the evening before he left for America. He said: 'I really think of this place, of this room, as home in England.' We were all rather sad and moved at the goodbyes: it was curiously as if we were saying goodbye for ever – though that wasn't the case at all, for Christopher came back to London several times in the next few years. But there was one significant difference: Bill Caskey no longer came with him, for Christopher had started a new relationship. In 1953 he met two young men by the names of Bachardy, Ted and Don, and found himself falling in love with the younger brother, Don, who looked even younger than his eighteen years. The gap between Don and Christopher was thirty years, and many of Christopher's friends were of the opinion that such a gap would have been great even in Ancient Greece; in

---

* Alexis Rassine, the dancer.

twentieth-century California they felt he was taking a serious personal risk and jeopardizing their whole life-style. However, the feeling between them grew and developed, and became a permanent loving alliance. In *My Guru and his Disciple* Christopher writes that he didn't feel guilty about the difference in their ages, 'but I did feel awed by the emotional intensity of our relationship, right from its beginning: the strange sense of a fated, mutual discovery. I knew that, this time, I had really committed myself. Don might leave me, but I couldn't possibly leave him, unless he ceased to need me. This sense of a responsibility which was almost fatherly made me anxious but full of joy.'

XII

At the beginning of their relationship, Don had not decided what career he wanted to pursue, but by 1956 he had started going to art school, and soon discovered that he had a special talent for portrait drawings. He drew a large number of portraits of Christopher in all moods, and began to do drawings of Christopher's friends. They were popular, and he had very soon accumulated a large number of commissions, which were increased by his exhibitions in Los Angeles and in New York. He was a hard worker, and his energy and application were a stimulus to Christopher. In the autumn of 1955 they went on a trip together to Europe, with a visit on the way to see Paul Bowles* in Tangier, where Christopher first tried kif, with shattering results. He wrote about this experience in his 'Visit to Anselm Oakes', which was originally planned as part of his next novel, but was eventually cut out and published by itself in *Exhumations*. Oakes himself was supposed to be a study of

---

* The American musician and novelist.

Aleister Crowley,* not Paul Bowles. In England Christopher introduced Don to all his English friends and relations, who, unlike some of his Californian friends, showed no prejudice or hesitation in welcoming a relationship that was obviously making Christopher so happy.

Unfortunately, soon after they returned to America Don went down with hepatitis, and while nursing him Christopher caught it himself. They were neither of them serious cases, but they had to abjure alcohol for the whole of a year. As soon as they could they began to look for a more permanent home. Christopher first of all bought a house – the first he had ever actually owned – at 434 Sycamore Road, Santa Monica, at the bottom of the canyon. They lived there for three years, but then changed it for a house further up the side of the canyon, 145 Adelaide Drive, where they lived for the rest of Christopher's life. I first saw it in 1969 when I began my connection with the University of Texas, and stayed there several times in the seventies. It consisted of a large, welcoming sitting-room cum dining-room with a balcony looking out over the canyon and a glimpse of the ocean beyond on the left. Behind the sitting-room, hung with pictures that Christopher had begun to collect, were bedrooms and Christopher's study where he kept his books and worked most mornings or dictated to Don when they were working on a script together. Outside the house, as you came in, was the garage, part of which had been converted into a studio for Don. It was a quiet house, as there was not much traffic on Adelaide Drive, and the atmosphere restful for a writer and an artist to live in. The next house along the Drive belonged to Charles Laughton and Elsa Lanchester, and Christopher, always an admirer of Laughton's acting talents, struck up a close friendship with them. In 1960 they planned to work on a theatrical version of Plato's dialogues which was intended to be essentially a life of Socrates; unfortunately Laughton developed gall-bladder trouble in the middle of the work, and suffered a heart attack as well. He was never well enough to pick up the work again properly before his death in 1962, and so the Socrates

* The notorious satanist.

script had to join the by now rather numerous projects, plays and films Christopher had worked on but which never came to anything, mostly through bad luck or stupidity on the part of the film moguls.

XIII

*T*he *World in the Evening* was published in the summer of
1954, and was not very warmly received. I had seen it
in proof before, and had written to Christopher in
May trying to express my rather muted appreciation.

The arrival of the Boy Lamkin from your side of the
ocean, and the fact that I've read the proofs of *The World in the
Evening*, reminds me that it's high time I wrote to you. If I've
put it off again and again, it's partly because I've been hoping
a letter would come from you, telling me how you liked the
London Mag., which has been going to you regularly . . . . So
there.

I expect you've already had any amount of letters about
the production of *I am a Camera* over here. Beatrix and I and
Alexi all saw it together just before I went off to Italy, and
enjoyed it immensely. The audience – a curious, semi-smart
audience – obviously enjoyed it immensely too, and had
probably not read the book to compare it. For us, there was a
slight feeling that the book was not the play – no sense of *Berlin*
outside the room – but we all thought John Van Druten had

done a first-class job on it. Dorothy Tutin was enchanting, but *not*, to me at an rate, the Sally you created, too wistful and delicate altogether. I just couldn't take that charming actor Michael as 'Chris', as you, no one who knows you could, I believe: it was a strange distorting glass all the time. We're all hoping that the success here, and the accumulation of pounds sterling, will encourage you to take another trip over very soon. Please do come. For one thing, I'd like to consult you about my autobiography* before it gets printed: it's actually in the last stages now, and is beginning to be someone else's life already. I feel as if I'd been writing a novel about an entirely imaginary character. Did you, by the way, get the copy of *New World Writing* with the Hogarth bit in it? I asked Victor Weybright§ to send you a copy.

I've just been interrupted (I'm writing from the Cottage, where all the spring trees, the magnolias and cherries and Japanese azaleas are in flower) by Alexi, summoning me to see the success of his asparagus bed and the netting for the peas he's constructed. He's gardening like mad in this first burst of real spring weather, with Lottie# beside him, and sends you his love.

Christopher, my feelings are so mixed after a first reading of the proofs of *The World in the Evening*, that I don't know what to say. Perhaps it would be more sensible not to say anything until I've read it again, as I shall have to, as I want to. Because I think it's a wonderful achievement, with a skill in construction, a narrative flow, a freshness of style and observation that are *you* at the top of your form; I think the theme of sexual jealousy is wonderfully handled, Aunt Sarah a moving and convincing character, and so many scenes first-class – I shall say more about that later – but I'm bothered by something; perhaps it's the Americanization of your dialogue, perhaps it's the handling of the queer theme that doesn't seem properly objectivized. I may be wrong; I may find I'm wrong when I reread it; but I know you would want me to say quite frankly what I felt. I wish you'd tell me what Random House

* Vol.1 of Lehmann's autobiography, *The Whispering Gallery*, was published by Longmans in 1955.
§ The publisher of *New World Writing* – an American paperback series in imitation of *Penguin New Writing*.
# John Lehmann's Dog Carlotta.

objected to? It strikes me that Alan White is being courageous
– in Edward Montagu's England – as well as sensible in his
stand. Do tell me what your friends over there think. I have a
feeling I may be suffering from a kind of over-preparation – I
have waited and longed for this novel for fifteen years,
Christopher!

During the last six weeks I've been able to get back to the
autobiography, but until then – apart from my BBC
work – I've been entirely absorbed in the organization of the
London Magazine. I believe that now, with four numbers out,
people can see its shape and intention. I do so very much want
to know what you think. It has been very exciting, anxious,
absorbing for me; and we had an absolutely amazing kick-off,
with a circulation about three times what we expected at our
most sanguine. It seems to be settling down now to something
between 18,000 and 20,000 – far more than I ever hoped.
There's only one thing seriously wrong: no contribution from
you. Do please remember how much I want you to appear in
its pages. When do you finish your film job? How has it turned
out? I want all your news.

This letter inspired a long reply from him, rather apologetic
in tone. He wrote:

Of course I am deeply interested in your reactions to the
novel. They don't altogether surprise me. I have always felt
that there was something wrong with Stephen (Monk, not
Spender!). I suppose the truth is that I am such an essentially
autobiographical writer that I simply cannot manipulate an
I – character which isn't me. This American voice is truly a
problem. I think perhaps I should have taken much more
trouble to make Stephen talk more British or more American in
different parts of the book. The way *I* talk is such a mish-
mash – always was. I believe I still use locutions I caught from
Berthold Viertel and the Refugees, all mixed in with old-
fashioned British slang and modern American, which is
probably only ninety nine per cent correct. As for the queer
part, I am conscious of having idealized both Charles and Bob,
and, in another sense, Michael. Charles and Bob are idealized
for propaganda purposes. (We have a joke in the studio that if

you want to make a film about a Nisei, you always make him a Purple Heart soldier, a winner of the Congressional Medal of Honor, a Phi Beta Kappa, and on top of that he has a white mother, and his father was only half Japanese!) Michael is idealized in order to vent my spleen against wicked bisexuals who break the hearts of innocent queens and then go waltzing back to Wifey. Random House was chiefly bothered by the queer part, and I have toned it down greatly, but I evidently didn't succeed in curing it. Perhaps one never does, when one patches.

It was not 'idealization' that worried Christopher's friends in England about Charles and Bob, but something far more embarrassing.

In the same letter he told me that the 'Metro job' on Diane de Poitiers had been

huge fun, and my efforts seem to have made a real hit; so I am to go on and write the screenplay – having now concocted the story. I think it comes under the heading of permissible melodramatic camp. (I have stolen much from Balzac and Dumas.) Anyhow this means that I will be working at the Studio until around the end of August – thus, I fear, being prevented from writing the screenplay of *I am a Camera*, which I have been asked to do by Henry Cornelius, the director.

The *Diane* film was sabotaged, in Christopher's view, by the 'front office' refusing to choose any of the actors he wanted himself, with the result that it was a flop. A thousand pities, because he thought that his work had been worth while, and indeed one of the best jobs he had ever done; also, if he had been able to take on the job of turning *I am a Camera* into a film he might have been able to prevent what so horrified and angered him – the introduction of a love-affair between Sally and the Christopher character. It was bound to happen with himself absent, but he wrote to me in September 1955: 'For the record, I found it disgusting ooh-la-la near pornographic trash – a shameful exhibition.'

During the following years, he was much occupied with a life of Ramakrishna, which was heavy going for him; but he slogged on with it as he felt he owed it to his Swami to finish it. He had also been asked to select an anthology of *Great English Short Stories* for Dell: he chose thirteen writers, Conrad, Chesterton, George Moore, Wells, Forster, Kipling, Lawrence, Katherine Mansfield, Ethel Mayne, Robert Graves, Maugham, Pritchett and William Plomer. It was a good anthology, but would have been even better if copyright difficulties had not prevented him from adding Conan Doyle and Dylan Thomas, as was his original intention. He said in his Introduction:

> I have made no attempt here to be definitive – as they call it – to trace the development of the Short Story in the British Isles and select the best examples of its most important types. That is one kind of anthology; valuable for students, perhaps, but a weary and dreary job for the anthologist, since there is nothing in Life or Art so depressing as that which one admires but does not love – and how can one love what is utterly and unquestionably The Best? The other kind of anthology – the kind I have tried to make – is, or should be, autobiographical. I, the anthologist, must not waste time guessing what the reader's taste may be; I must boldly confess my own. The reader may not approve of it or of me, but at least my book will have a certain individuality . . . .'

Great English Short Stories was published in 1957.

> I don't know what to tell you about my novel. It has sort of stuck, and yet I could almost publish the bits. If I do, you shall have first refusal as far as England is concerned. I promised you that already . . . . Am in fact full of ideas but short of money and must make some quick. So Don and I are off to New York tomorrow morning, to nose around there. And incidentally to see Stephen, Wystan, John Gielgud etc . . . . I ought to come to England this summer – aside from everything else, to see my mother who has passed her 90th birthday and is said to have recovered about 90% from her stroke. I shall come if I can manage it financially.

The novel was what he still called his 'Mexican fantasy novel'. Like so many of his books, it went through a large number of transmogrifications, false starts and rearrangements, but by the time he wrote to me in June 1959 it had taken the shape we know as *Down There on a Visit*, and he had sent me the first episode, 'Mr Lancaster', for separate publication in the *London Magazine*. It seemed to me to recapture some of his old spirits and ease of telling, and I wrote enthusiastically accepting it.

My dear Christopher – You can scarcely imagine what a surprise and joy it was to me to have your letter, followed so swiftly, 48 hours later in fact, by the packet from Edward containing 'Mr Lancaster'. I swallowed it in one big, immediate, gulp, and can only say Hip-hop-hooray! If it weren't for the studied distancing effected by your apostrophes to Youth, it might have been done at the same time as *Goodbye to Berlin*. You are in *vintage* form, and I couldn't be more pleased and excited to have it for the *London Mag*. Is it really autobiography? Does it slip into an hitherto invisible gap between *Lions and Shadows* and *Goodbye to Berlin*? Or is it just skilfully concocted to seem like that? Anyway, as it is a part of what was originally planned as a continuous novel, I can only suppose that all the other parts are of the same epoch: I just can't wait to read them. I had to put it down several times because I laughed so much: and then I felt how well you sprung the surprise on your reader of his suicide and the revelation of him having been *proud* of you. I shall put it into the very first number of the *LM* I can, without a word cut, occupying most of the number. But when will that be, with this bloody printing strike going on? My August number (due mid-July) is all ready to be printed, page proofs passed; my September number's main features announced in it. If it only lasts three weeks, I can do a bit of shifting around, and everything will be all right; if longer, we're in the soup. That everyone else is too doesn't somehow console me. And of course books will all be jammed into one hectic period of nine weeks or so just before Christmas, my own book – *I am my Brother** – included. And as Longmans are publishing for Reynal, that goes for the American edition too.

* The second volume of Lehmann's autobiography, published in 1960 by Longmans.

My heart is in turmoil again, and I am more bewildered than ever before by the fact that 'happiness' is torment and hell.

My fondest wishes to Don – I'm so glad to hear he's making a success in the new venture – and very much love to yourself.

Christopher replied:

I'm simply delighted that you liked 'Mr Lancaster' so much. There are certain things in it I expect to change when the whole book is done, but I had better not try until I see how it relates to the other parts. Edward (Upward), also, was enthusiastic: so I feel greatly reassured.

Yes – It is autobiographical. Mr Lancaster was Basil Fry, a cousin of mine, who was British Consul at Bremen. I paid him a visit at just that time. He didn't commit suicide but died, poor devil, at some ghastly post in South America. I think it was a port in the nitrate desert of Northern Chile. I don't think he had any particular feeling for me. And there was no episode with Waldemar.

The idea of the novel is really best expressed by my old title, The Lost. I have also been playing with something resembling 'Là-bas', and thought of 'Down There on a Visit'. But, actually, this is an account of four separate visits – not to hell, exactly, but to people who are living in private hells of different kinds; not entirely grim, however, and not always alone. Only two characters appear in all four episodes; Waldemar and me, at different ages. You might say, Waldemar is Heinz, but with many alterations.

In the next episode, he and I go down to Greece, right after the time in Berlin, in May 1933, and there encounter a lot of people living on an island, with an Englishman named Ambrose as their leader. This episode is really very broad farce, but with an underlying horror. Then the third episode will be in London during the Munich crisis. Waldemar will be there, living with an Englishwoman I've always wanted to write about. This episode is vaguest in conception so far, but I came across a diary I kept at that time which had many valuable hints in it. Then the last episode will take place in Santa

Monica, during the last year of the war, and it will be all about Denny Fouts and yoga and drugs. And there will be an epilogue after the war, about 1952, in Berlin when Denny is dying; and I meet Waldemar again as a middle-aged married man. I hope and think this episode will be the one which gets down nearest to the nerve, as Francis Bacon puts it.

But this epilogue was never written, or at any rate was not published with the book. He wrote to me about the very last stages in its long-drawn-out birth in December 1960, just before Christmas: 'Yes, the novel is finished, and indeed largely revised. However the last longest and most horrendous section, nearly as long as *The Memorial*, isn't! Heaven alone knows what it is like, let alone what you all will think of it; I can only tell you that I feel far fewer misgivings than I did about Whirled in the Evenink. This, for better or worse, is *me*.'

I read *Down There on a Visit* in July of the following year, and wrote to Christopher after 'having gradually abandoned everything else: tribute to your witchery, as powerful as ever. When I got to the end, I could hardly believe I'd read a book of 100,000 words. In fact, I enjoyed it immensely, and found myself laughing over ''Mr Lancaster'' just as much as – if not more than – when I first read it.' I then launched into some critical observations, in the usual way between us.

Mr Lancaster seems to me far the most successfully realised of the four pieces; partly because Mr Lancaster is fully developed himself as a comic-tragic character, partly because the narrator is seen in the perspective of time by a second Isherwood. 'Ambrose' is my next favourite. I think you convey the utterly bizarre quality of the island colony wonderfully well. At the same time I think more might have been stated – or seen. Without indecency, Ambrose's relations with the boys could have been made more explicit. As it is, in fact, they scarcely exist at all. And I am a little uncomfortable about the narrator-Waldemar relationship: I just can't believe it without sex as the bond. And yet 'you' go out of your way to say that 'you' didn't love him *personally*. (I am much less critical of 'Ambrose' after several re-readings, because I am struck by the sheer marvellousness of the writing.) The 'Waldemar' episode which follows it, came nearest to disappointing me. It seemed to me too much taken up with the details of your Munich crisis – and not seen in perspective, either . . . . It is full of dread and bitterness about England, the times etc., but suffers from too little character drawing. In Paul I felt the lack of 'perspective' even more, though it is a far more fascinating piece. Partly it is due, I think to the fact that Yoga plays so important a part, and you want to – or have to – preach about it. But more, I believe it is due to not having got yourself properly outside the Paul-narrator relationship. Every now and then I found myself missing the *second* Isherwood rather badly. Why did the narrator find Paul so utterly intriguing? Again without the indication of sexual tastes in common it's difficult to be entirely convinced; because Paul just doesn't seem worth it . . . .

Looking over all this, it strikes me as an extreme case of cantankerous old editor Lehmann finding as much fault as possible. But I think you know me well enough to know how such criticism can coexist within a general feeling of delight and admiration. And my objections to Paul may of course be because I'm non-conducting to Gerald Heard mysticism.

Though not going as far as the *New York Times* critic who found Paul 'despicable', I have never been able to take him on Christopher's valuation. But I know younger readers who delight in the whole book and put it on the par with *Goodbye to Berlin*. With *Prater Violet*, I certainly consider 'Mr Lancaster' and 'Ambrose' the best things that Christopher wrote in fiction after the translation to America, even the much-admired *A Single Man* which, with its complete change of technique, came next.

XIV

Towards the end of October 1959, Christopher sent me the typescript of a long short story which he had been telling me about for some time. It was called 'Afterwards' and was about 20,000 words long – a length he had always excelled in, but in other ways it was very different from anything else he ever wrote (or at any rate anything I ever saw). It has never been published, though stories in the same genre have been posthumously published for E.M. Forster and Lytton Strachey.

The story is told in the first person by a homosexual young man who has recently lost his lover in a flying accident. He is obsessed by the memory of this lover, Tom, and feels he can never pick up the threads of life again. Then one day, at the gym, he sees two young men 'who are almost too beautiful together', Forrest and Leonard. He starts a friendship with them, and they begin spending two or three evenings a week together, though there is nothing sexual at this stage in their relationship. One evening, however, the two young men are unable to get home and spend the evening in the narrator's flat, where he sees them make love together, and is much excited by the scene. Then, a few days later, Forrest comes alone to the narrator, and tells him that he has met someone who knows him and knows about Tom, who hasn't been mentioned before. Forrest shows an immense curiosity about their affair, and manages to persuade the narrator to show him the albums of photographs he has kept of Tom and himself together. When Forrest has gone home, the narrator finds that one nude photograph of himself and Tom is missing. Forrest finally confesses to having stolen the photograph because he was so excited by it. Very soon the narrator and Forrest, almost inevitably, start an affair together, but the narrator is not happy about it, and goes off to New York. When he comes back, he finds that Forrest has started a promiscuous life, and has left Leonard. It is scarcely a surprise that Leonard and the narrator should thereupon fall in to one another's arms; and the story ends with them planning a new life together.

Christopher solves the problem of language in this story by imagining the narrator as a rather coarse-grained American homosexual who is acquainted with all the current slang for any-thing queers do with one another – and they do most things imaginable. This works most of the time, but at the expense of any suggestion that there is any loving tenderness in any of their activities. In fact, the story steers very close to pornography, with the organs of the actors always enormous and their emissions unceasing. But the story is redeemed from that by the extreme cunning of the telling, in particular when Forrest is revealed to have stolen the photograph, a subtle turn as good as anything imagined by Isherwood elsewhere in his work. As soon as I had read it, I wrote to him praising the psychological inventiveness of that episode, but also saying that there was an element of erotic fantasy that was dangerously near getting out of hand running right through it; in particular, I doubted whether the ending was entirely plausible, as leading to a new life-long relationship between the narrator and Leonard. It seemed to me (and still seems to me) a little hurried, a little scamped for that consum-mation; almost as if the author had got bored with his characters and their endless interchange of beds. He never said to me that he wanted to revise it, so one must assume that the text he sent me is as he finally wished it to be – if in fact he envisaged it as being published at all even as a posthumous work.

Christopher faced me with a considerable problem about showing it to other people. In his letter of 18 October he said merely that:

> If you like it, you are absolutely free to show it around to any suitable readers. I would suggest Morgan Forster, just because he has let me see some things of his in this genre from time to time; but that's a matter for your decision. I couldn't in any case send him a copy direct to Cambridge, as I don't know the setup there and its arrival might somehow embarrass him. Explain this to him if you *do* show him your copy.

I was extremely reluctant to send it by post anywhere, or indeed to let it go out of my keeping at all. So eventually I decided to let certain selected people read it in my house. But I was prepared to make an exception for Morgan, if necessary: I would take it down to Cambridge myself in my car, if he was not going to be available in town in the near future.

XV

*D*own *There on a Visit* was published in 1962. Christopher was rather more wounded by some of the reviews than he liked to admit, particularly by one written by a London friend who specially asked if Christopher would like him to review it – and then slammed it. Christopher didn't think that was ethical: in his view if that friend hadn't liked it, he should have passed it on to someone else and then written to the author to explain.

Isn't that your idea of the proper procedure or am I being unreasonable? Morgan, who didn't much care for the book, took the trouble to write and tell me so, and I was very touched. He would *never* have stated his opinion in print.

Over here, I've so far had three favorable reviews in papers that count; one unfavorable, and that was sheer puritan horror. A lot of minor reviewers have been horrified too, and a lot have been favorable. But I have found very little understanding of what the book's about – at least, as I see it. To me, the book's about alienation, aggression, persecution-complexes, failure of communication between individuals 'in the sea of life enisled', and the way certain personalities wriggle out of all the categories people try to put them into. It is *not*, in any important way, about sex of any kind. That's quite incidental.

I have just had a new idea for a novel, a short one. I'm very excited about it, but it will be difficult to do. Very subtle. And, believe it or not, clean as a whistle.

Don is fine. His show in New York was a huge success. He may have one here, but probably not till the fall. I think he'll be having another in the East during the summer. He is working hard and sends his love.

I'm working hard, too. On the Ramakrishna biography, which I want to finish up as soon as possible. And then I'm teaching at one of the local colleges, twice a week. I have, among other things, what's called a Creative Writing class. You should just hear some of the stories the students write! I was reading one of them aloud last week to the class, and the dialogue was such (Marine Corps style) that I was afraid someone from the outside would hear and I'd be fired!

The 'idea for a novel' was what eventually became *A Single Man*, but once again after many transmutations. It was originally called 'An Englishwoman', and the chief character was to be an Englishwoman who has married a GI and then finds herself lost in California. In the final, published version, the Englishwoman is reduced to a minor role and the lead is taken by an English lecturer, the central experience of whose past life has been an affair with Jim, a young American homosexual who has been killed in an accident. It has been very much praised, and is thought by many to be Christopher's masterpiece, at any rate of his post-war American writings. Technically it is a new departure, being a third-person autobiographical exercise, with the time-span reduced to twenty-four hours, a device he had never tried before, but he shows immense skill in coping with its challenge.

At the time he was writing it, he was, as he indicated in his letter to me, working as a professor in the University of California at Santa Barbara, which gave him much fresh material for the new novel, used with witty and sardonic effect. I think that anyone who has been through the experience of teaching English literature at an American college (see Afterword) will find the description of a class on an Aldous Huxley novel uncannily life-like and indeed humorous in just the right quiet way.

I wrote to him about *A Single Man* in May 1964:

> My dear Christopher, I'm off to Switzerland the moment this holiday weekend is over (invited by something grand-sounding called the Pro Helvetia Foundation which seems to know, with cunning insight, just exactly when a middle-aged literary gent needs this kind of morale-booster), but I felt I must write before in order to tell you, at least first time over, how much I've enjoyed *A Single Man*, the proofs of which John Cullen* was kind enough to send me. Of course I wanted more, much more, and damn the unities (perhaps because I've just been re-reading *Edwin Drood* and see everything stretching out with utterly fascinating complexity into the unknown), but I think you've done it beautifully. I think Kenny is marvellously real, and the whole tone, the new tone, is superb. You're funny in a new way, a sour, sardonic, merciless way, and it seems to me just to suit the person you've become. Years ago, just before you went to South America, you said to me you'd resolved never to be funny again; that the one thing people paid you out for in the end was entertaining them. That really meant you'd put paid to Herr Issyvoo; but *The World in the Evening* didn't quite get the new voice right (in my opinion), and in some ways *Down There on a Visit* was a bit of a throw-back. Now I think you're right on target; though of course you *are* entertaining, but in a new way that cuts and doesn't give a damn about being kind.
>
> Well, I shall probably write more, when I've read it again and properly digested it; but meanwhile all my congratulations.
>
> I'm down at the cottage with Alexi now back from S. Africa, and Rudy (my golden retriever), and the weather is sublime and the rhododendrons and azaleas are bursting out everywhere and the birds singing like mad. (I saw one thrush trying out all its trills and cadenzas while it hunted for worms in the lawn – as if Joan Sutherland were to practice her arias

* John Cullen worked for Methuen who published *A Single Man* in 1964.

while shopping in a super-market.) My 'Christ the Hunter'*
has been recorded by the BBC, and I do believe added up to
something – I won't say more. When I get back from
Switzerland I've got to face up to selling No. 31.

In these years Christopher lost two friends who had become
very dear to him, Aldous Huxley and Charles Laughton; as well
as his mother, who died at the age of ninety-one in June 1960.
Huxley's death, which occurred on the same day as President
Kennedy's assassination in Dallas, was not followed by any
religious or other celebration in America, except a walk by a group
of his friends along the highway that he had taken every day as
long as his health allowed it. In London a packed gathering
assembled at the Friends' Meeting House where his brother Julian
delivered a deep moving address, and Yehudi Menuhin played
the violin. Laughton, who died also of cancer in December 1962,
was much missed by Christopher, who wrote to me of his death:
'It was a long weary death, the most painful I have ever had to
watch. Either they should find a cure for cancer or finish them
off; it's too awful and useless. Peggy [my sister Beatrix] will be
especially sad, I expect.' I think that Christopher and Laughton
might have become successful collaborators in many things beside
the planned Socrates film, as they enjoyed the same jokes and
had the same basic attitude to homosexuality. But it was not to be.

In December 1963 Christopher was persuaded by Swami
Prabhavananda to accompany him and two other of his followers
on a brief visit to Calcutta, in order to attend the centenary
celebrations for Vivekananda.§ His experiences there helped him
to complete the weary task of his *Ramakrishna and his Disciples*,
a duty work vetted chapter by chapter by the Ramakrishna Order,
and published without any enthusiasm on his part in April 1965.
But the visit also, more satisfactorily, gave him an idea how to
organize the new novel which was already stirring in his mind
and in due course became *A Meeting by the River*. But before he
started work on this, his final novel, he was deflected by a
suggestion from an English admirer that he should collect his

* *Christ the Hunter* was published in 1965 by Eyre & Spottiswoode.
§ A Vedanta swami.

stray articles, book reviews and other miscellaneous writings, which he envisaged in some sense as part of his autobiography. It was published with the wry title of *Exhumations* in 1966. Though inevitably uneven in interest, it is full of plums and essential reading for the Isherwood enthusiast. He was further deflected by new engagements in the film studios, when Tony Richardson agreed to direct a film from Evelyn Waugh's *The Loved One* with Christopher and Terry Southern working on the script together. Someth:ng went wrong with the collaboration, and the film was not a success. He also prepared a script for Tony Richardson on Carson McCullers's *Reflections in a Golden Eye*; but Richardson backed out, and the film was produced by John Huston from another script. He prepared a third script for Richardson from Marguerite Duras's novel *The Sailor from Gibraltar*, which was even unluckier. In fact the long months in the studios brought him nothing but temporary financial help. In his letters to me between June 1964 and April 1965, he refers frequently to the books he was preparing and his script-writing. In April 1965 he wrote:

I hardly expect you to like my Ramakrishna book (he didn't send it to me). It is too 'party line'. Perhaps I shall be able to convey my relation to all that more vividly when I write something exclusively autobiographical. I probably told you that I am doing a book of bits and pieces, called *Exhumations*? Methuen is supposed to publish it in the autumn. And now I am trying another (short) novel. Quite a new departure, all letters and diary entries. But I'm very dubious if it will work. It takes place in India in a monastery, and is about two brothers. One of them is just about to take his final vows as a Hindu monk, and the other comes to visit him, simply horrified but determined to be broad-minded. And all hell (on a tiny scale) breaks loose! Doesn't that sound like the least-likely-to-succeed story of the year?

He added: 'You will have to watch *The Loved One* narrowly to catch a glimpse of me! There are actually a couple, during John Gielgud's funeral, unless they have been cut out at the last moment.' The glimpses were not cut out, and Christopher can still be seen in the film, in his only appearance in a movie prepared by himself. By May 1966 I had read and reviewed *Exhumations*, and Christopher wrote to me: 'I was really delighted and moved by your review of *Exhumations*. Not only that you liked it and wrote about it so perceptively, but also because I felt so much warmth of friendship beneath what you wrote. Altogether, the reception of the book has been a happy surprise to me . . . . No American reviews are out yet.'

During the sixties and seventies our relationship changed to some extent, because Christopher visited England more frequently and because I began to visit America on long stints as a lecturer and visiting professor. The result was many fewer letters between us and meetings instead in London or California. During the first half of 1961 Don enrolled in the Slade for six months, and Christopher came over as often as his work, in particular his courses at Santa Barbara, permitted. He and Don went for a holiday in the South of France, and then when Don had finished at the Slade he had to stay in Europe some weeks longer to deal with various commissions for portrait drawings which were steadily accumulating. During the mid-sixties Christopher started the preparatory work on a book about his parents, *Kathleen and Frank*, which had germinated in his mind after his mother's death. The research for this book completely altered his view of his father, dominated before now by his mother's fixation with her husband as a hero-figure after his death in battle. This heroic ideal had become the mainspring of Christopher's revolt against family and country. He now came to see his father as a frustrated artist, always longing to escape from the claims of his military calling.

In the spring of 1967, after apologizing for the unusual writer's block which had prevented him writing letters, he wrote:

now I'm happy to say I'm off to the races – I have written seventy-some pages. What the book is really about, I don't know yet; and whether what it is about is in the least interesting is another moot question. Perhaps the only interesting thing will be the construction, as I shall dart about back and forth in time. There will be a lot of research to do in England anyway, before I can produce a finished version. I have to read at least fifteen to twenty years of my Mother's day-to-day diaries, and endless correspondence, and also delve into my ancestor Judge Bradshaw's past. If only I could prove he was queer!

Your autobiography is so fascinating, and such a picture of your time. I read a review of it (I mean of *Proposition** by Peter Quennell (?)) in which he seemed to object that you are so kind to everyone, as though this were a fault. Intelligent comment does *not* have to be malicious – how few people know that nowadays. I was interested to read the same thing said – but approvingly – in a review in the *London Magazine* of the Cocteau book about people he has known. I adore Cocteau and it is true, I think. Your reference to him is very amusing.

Meanwhile, in the middle of the long, slow grind of *Kathleen and Frank*, Christopher had written 'the least-likely-to-succeed story of the year' in three drafts, the last being finished in the spring of 1966 – though even that draft was altered after criticism by John Yale, one of the two followers of Vedanta who had become Swamis after the visit to India. *A Meeting by the River* was published in the spring of 1967, and is Christopher's most ambitious attempt to write 'the religious novel', ending as it does with a vision in which the brother who is becoming a Hindu monk feels himself mystically united with his 'guru' – the idea of which had obsessed Christopher for so many years. I cannot say that this mystical climax made me sympathetically disposed to the work, but I recognize that it is a work of extreme subtlety and complexity, in which the relationship between the two brothers, Patrick and Oliver, is explored in all its actual and potential aspects so that the reader cannot be certain whether they are intended to be in love with one another or two sides of one deeply divided person. What I could and do admire is the skill of the story-telling in which letters and diary extracts and reflections are alternated, and the shock of surprise when it is revealed that Patrick has a homosexual lover, Tom, whom he is thinking about and passionately remembering as his aeroplane goes on humming through the night on the way to India. What I am still unable to take is the letter of rejection which Patrick sends to Tom after

* *The Ample Proposition*, the third volume of Lehmann's autobiography, published in 1966 by Eyre & Spottiswoode.

his drunken telephone-call, which seems to me disgustingly priggish and false, particularly in its advice to Tom to try marriage – to a woman.

I must admit that I have never read the re-writing of *A Meeting by the River* as a play, which Christopher prepared with Don in 1968, and is said by some critics to be a considerable artistic improvement on the novel. It has been produced in America, but so far has not been published. They also re-wrote it again as a film-script, making further alterations of emphasis; but it has never been made into a movie. In his letter to me in the spring of 1967, Christopher had added at the end:

> I absolutely have to come to England before too long, so I look forward to seeing you. It is so nice that through all these years we have never really lost touch with each other. I wish I could say that for all of my old friends. Of course, in some instances, there are good reasons. We had Wystan to stay the other day, and there too, I was happy to feel that underneath the great structure of his public image the friend was still absolutely there.

Our friendship had lasted thirty-five years when he wrote that letter, and was still as warm and cloudless on my side as it was on his. When I first knew him he had only one novel to his credit, *All the Conspirators*, which attracted little enough notice when first published, and only sold a few hundred copies. During the thirty-five years of our friendship all that was to change phenomenally. His story 'The Nowaks' in *New Writing* No. 1 was spotted as the work of a writer of style, wit and warmth. *The Memorial*, the first novel he published with the Hogarth Press, had aroused my enthusiasm when I read it in typescript: it had equally little success in sales, but attracted the attention of the serious critics. The second Hogarth novel, *Mr Norris Changes Trains*, was a deservedly unqualified success and showed that this new author had an exceptional gift for comic characterization and skill in telling a story. With the little book *Sally Bowles*, which was originally intended as a contribution for *New Writing*, he was away. It was probably the most popular of his stories, being made – as I've said – into a play and a film, and then into a musical before it finally appeared as the film *Cabaret*. His migration to the USA which came shortly after, seemed to set him back for a bit, but after the partial failure of his next novel, *Goodbye to Berlin*, he showed himself back on the top of his form with *Prater Violet*, and was already being talked of as the hope of the English novel, with the future in his hands.

From very early on we had shared our most intimate secrets, and rejoiced with one another over our successes – whether in our writings or other public ventures – and over our special friendships. Although he knew my reservations about his Vedanta beliefs, he never pushed them under my nose, nor did I ever during the war question his new-found pacifism even though I deeply regretted his absence from the profound experiences we were undergoing – an absence which I feared would create a gulf between us. But it didn't. If I had doubts about any of his literary schemes I stated them as frankly as I could, and he never appeared to resent my criticisms because I think my fundamental love of and faith in his work was always apparent to him. I could always count on him for sympathy and encouragement in anything I undertook myself whether it was for the books I was writing or for more editorial ventures or my publishing struggles, or, later on, my attempts to convey something of my values about literature to young American students. When I think of him now, I think first of the pleasure that I always felt when he came to see me or I visited him, his bubbling zany wit and his free-wheeling imaginative gift for turning any situation that one discussed with him, however troubling it might seem to one, into absurdity and fantasy. A friend in a million, a friend of the greatest rarity. I don't know what a life that has had its ups and downs would have been like without him.

AFTERWORD

I n 1969 I started several years of lecturing and visiting
professorship, at various American universities, starting with
the University of Texas at Austin, which had a special
attraction for me as it housed the Humanities Research Center,
in which all my *New Writing* and *London Magazine* papers were
collected. During the course of the seventies I also did seminars
or terms at the University of California, San Diego, Berkeley
College in San Francisco and Emory College in Atlanta. As a
result, and owing to the fact that Christopher was frequently
visiting England during these years, the letters between us became
much rarer, but I have been able to supplement them with
occasional diary entries. By 1980 Christopher had developed a
strong aversion from writing letters except when he had to for
business purposes, and almost all the communications between
us were by telephone, speedy and reliable if a little more
expensive.

Adelaide Drive, 24 January 1968 (letter from C.I. to J.L.).

I am still working on the preliminary copying and cutting of the mass of my Mother's diaries and Father's letters. There is a book in them, maybe two books when all the other material is included; neither of them novels, of course. If I do write another novel, it will be something deliberately unsensational and rather sentimental; all taking place on the silver wedding-day of two late-middle-aged queens, one of them working at the telephone company and the other at the gas company; they live in a dreadful little home in some dreadful part of Los Angeles and have a spaniel named Jeanette Macdonald and are very dull and happy . . . .

Incidentally, as regards *Cabaret*, I dearly wish I was making a fortune out of it; but so many cuts are being taken out of the pie that my slice is small indeed. If Auden and I had written the book, as originally planned, maybe we'd have made a fortune! . . .

Cornwall Gardens, 14 May 1969 (letter from J.L. to C.I.).

The ceremony of unveiling the memorial to Byron in Westminster Abbey, last week, put me in mind of that dinner in March at your house, which I enjoyed so much. I felt I must write to you about it. William* made an excellent oration, very much to the point, not too solemn at all: afterwards, in the Jerusalem Chamber, when I told him about Vergil Th. and his opera,§ he said he thought perhaps his speech ought to be included as the final aria . . . . The Dean was very funny, unconsciously: he kept on saying (at least if you listened between the lines) that he and the Chapter knew that Byron was a very licentious fellow, that they had no intention of giving in to the 'promiscuous society', but after all in 1969 one ought to be grown up enough to distinguish between the life and the poetry, etc., etc. The ghost of the Noble Lord stalked out with a great guffaw of rage at that moment. If I hadn't been such a hopeless coward, I would have got up and recited one of Byron's poems to his boy-friend, the 'To Thyrza' poems perhaps.

I must thank you for sending on that great fat letter from my marvellous young friend in Austin, Texas. You may be amused to hear what he wrote: 'Please give my affectionate good wishes to Christopher Isherwood. He would not be surprised to hear that to me – and to many of my friends – he has, for a number of years, been "Christopher" – a first-name basis.' And lots more. There. He is only 24.

---

* William Plomer.
§ Virgil Thomson, the American composer who wrote the opera *Lord Byron*.

Do please write to me, and tell me how all your dramatic projects go. And give my fondest love to yourself, and to Don, as always.

You remember that epic Indian book you let me read? Well, Kenny Martin* the other day produced the second volume, about the cowboys. I chuckled myself silly. But he told me that a young American friend of his had told him, *perfectly seriously*, 'Do you know who is really the author? It's a poet, by the name of W. Auden . . .' *Honi soit.*

*Kenneth Martin, the novelist and a friend of John Lehmann.

Adelaide Drive, 1 June 1969 (letter from C.I. to J.L.).

. . . Don sends his love. We are very busy on the film story of
Cabaret and hope they will see it our way. Other projects, such
as our play adapted from *A Meeting by the River* and our
proposed trip to Australia aren't definite but look somewhat
hopeful. The *Black Girl* adaptation had a very successful run but
hasn't yet found any other offers.* The musical version of *The
Dog Beneath the Skin* looks as if it may get a tryout in San
Francisco before too long. In our spare time Don paints and I
crawl along with my Family book – that will become more fun
in later chapters but oh God I am *praying* for the end of the
Boer War!. . .

(Christopher had discussed the part in his book about the Boer
War with me because my father – who became a Liberal MP
in 1905-6 – had been politically involved in the controversies.)

* Isherwood wrote a dramatized adaptation of Bernard Shaw's story 'The
Adventures of the Black Girl in her Search for God' in 1968.

Adelaide Drive, 19 September 1969 (letter from C.I. to J.L.).

    I am only just beginning to answer letters after our trip to Tahiti, Samoa, New Zealand, Australia, Honolulu, which was one of the happiest and most fascinating trips I have ever made in my life. In fact we both loved it . . . . We rendezvoused with Tony Richardson, watching him making his film, met and adored Mick Jagger – he is a very unusual person with great style, the perfect balance of introvert-extrovert, very funny, perfectly serious when he is serious, a 'gentleman' according to my mother's rating, almost entirely without affectation and, it seems, vanity. You would never guess, meeting him, all that he publicly is. Well, anyhow, as a result of our talks with Tony, we are now engaged in producing a screenplay of *I, Claudius* which Tony want to film next. It is about the hardest thing I have ever worked on in movies, but very stimulating. That's why I haven't been answering letters. And there are many weeks of work ahead . . .

(The film of *I, Claudius* was eventually given another script-writer and another director.)

Diary entry: San Diego, Tuesday 3 November 1970.

On Friday at lunch-time, suddenly Christopher was there, with Don (silky silver hair in page-boy cut, a new development) beside him. My friend Morris was immensely excited to meet them, C. at his sweetest with him; in fact all three got on wonderfully well together, in spite of Morris's obvious shyness and anxiety. Don had brought with him photo-reproductions of some of his drawings as a present to me: I chose one of C. himself (a very good full-length standing one), one of Morgan, and a head of Wystan (both looking rather serious, even fierce – as Don's portraits are apt to be). He also brought some nudes of boys as a special present; but can I put them up on my walls?

C. talked a great deal about his new book on the subject of his father and mother, which whetted my appetite. Still no news of his play being put on in London*, a disappointment he bears bravely. We gave them goulash, jointly prepared. We all went off to the zoo, watched the lemurs, walked through the fantastic aviaries, wondered at the aardvark (the ant-eater), and the pygmy hippopotamus. Then they took us home, and off they went back to Santa Monica. C. on the waggon entirely. Not a drop of alcohol. We discussed E.M.F.'s will, and the plans for publishing *Maurice*. And the fate of the destroyed Mortmere stories: C. said the fact was they weren't nearly as good as 'The Railway Accident', so one shouldn't grieve overmuch.

---

* A production of *A Meeting by the River* had been proposed by stage director Clifford Williams.

On Sunday evening, as Sue hadn't seen the aquarium and Morris wanted to be beside the ocean, we drove down to the Scripps Institute,* and then on to Anthony's by the waterfront, where we gave Sue a sea-food dinner; and so home. In the aquarium, I, laughing at some of the fish who seemed to stare at us, sitting on their fins like race-goers on shooting sticks, said: 'They're exactly like my students.' And Morris, quick as a flash, said, 'That's why they're called a school.'

Much telephoning between Christopher and myself, and writing between Mark Schorer§ and myself; the result of which is that I am going up to lecture at Berkeley on Monday 23rd, and will spend the night with C. and Don at Santa Monica on the way.

* The Scripps Institute of Oceanography.
§ The American writer and critic.

Diary entry: 26 November – Thanksgiving.

Last week-end was a big break in my routine here. First of all to Los Angeles, where C. met me, and I stayed the night at their Santa Monica home. Before going to the canyon, we lunched in the town, and talked again of C's new work about his parents, and the discoveries about L.S.W.* Then to the canyon, where Don emerged and immediately dragged me off to be drawn before the light failed. Afterwards he went out to dinner, and C. and I were left to talk endlessly together, though this was broken by a visit to Elsa Lanchester – a few yards away down the canyon – very affectionate and gentle ('on her best behaviour' said C.) and reminiscing much about the early days with Beatrix. C. and I talked a great deal about E.M.F.'s literary remains, the edition of *Maurice* which is to come out under P.N. Furbank's editorship – C. very irritated by the failure of communication with England, with Furbank's hopeless copies, and the difficulty of persuading him that E.M.F.'s notes to *Maurice* should be published with it. I gather that Morgan re-wrote it once more *after* he had shown it to me (and others) in the early fifties. C. then showed me an extraordinary long short story Morgan had written between twelve and fifteen years before his death, also on a homosexual theme, of quite extraordinary power and depth ('The Other Boat'). I was, I must admit, overwhelmed. Later, as I was looking through the books on Morgan in Christopher's library, he said: 'Of course all those books have got to be re-written. Unless you start with the fact that he was homosexual, nothing's any good at all.'

* Leonard Woolf.

The next day, C. and Don insisted on driving me up to Santa Barbara, to have lunch with two artist friends of theirs, Bill and Paul. A delicious occasion, with marvellous ham pie and asparagus cooked by Paul, and much viewing of artistic works . . . . Bill gave me a drawing, and the generosity of the gesture compelled me to embrace him for it . . . . Owing to a muddle C. had made about airlines, we had to drive back to Los Angeles for me to catch my plane to San José, Don driving like a demon along the crowded freeways, between the sombre barren mountains in the gathering twilight – we reached it with twenty minutes to go. C. confessed he could hardly bear to answer letters nowadays. And also told me that all his affairs would be in Don's hands after his death.

Diary entry: 16 December.

I do not really believe in these 'Creative Writing' courses as they are taught and so popular now in the USA universities. I felt doubts at the beginning, and now that my course is completed here I feel my doubts confirmed. I *cannot* see what is gained by the most popular way of handling them: all the students reading out their own poems in class, a sort of mass confessional, and then tearing one another to pieces. It is somehow ridiculous, even if the 'teacher' steers the discussion. I have spent so many years of my life discussing with authors *one by one*, and privately, where I think them good, where I think they go wrong, what line to pursue; and I am certain that's the only way. What is possible *in class* is to take a well-known poem, group of poems, or a short story, and ask each student to analyse, give reasons for liking or disliking, and discuss with the others, the 'teacher' finally developing (and arguing) his point of view. In that way certainly we have had the most successful general sessions.

I take away the feeling that the young in this country are bitter, unsatisfied, disaffected from the way things are run, the way things are going in their huge, unsettled country, that has so little to anchor it to life – traditions, history, the slow evolution of settled communities . . . .

On the long journey by air from London to Austin (January) I read P.N. Furbank's article in *Encounter* on E.M.F. How odd to present such a fascinating character so dully. He is critical of Joe's article, and yet Joe is nearer the truth, and brings out one wonderful side of Morgan: his habit of writing, out of the blue, to his friends, praising and encouraging. I have been the lucky recipient of more than one such letter. And if I think, in recollecting, of Morgan, the pictures that always come to mind first, are of his gaiety. I see him sitting on my sofa, in my library at Egerton Crescent, convulsed with merriment at some absurd joke or situation.

It is extraordinary, how I have felt a wonderful lift of the heart at being back in Austin. There is something about the air (not merely the warmth for mid-winter) – there is something about the light – which stimulates me and flushes me with happiness, almost inducing euphoria. I found a class, scheduled to consist of forty-six students, awaiting me for my 'Nonsense' course, with at least a dozen more trying to get in. Two or three of them complained out loud that they had been refused enrolment, told that the class was full. At which I said without thinking, 'What nonsense! The class is full when the room is full' – to be greeted with thunderous applause. And their responsiveness to the preliminary, testing examples of nonsense I gave them was enthusiastic and immediate. My graduate seminar was equally delightful in quite a different way: a group of a dozen students in a small room, all intelligent and – so it seemed to me – intensely interested in the subject, especially the Bloomsbury Group and Virginia.

To visit Warren in his office, finding him in rather sombre mood, gloomy about the prospects for the HRC*, not un-critical by any means of the three whose resignations have caused all the uproar. I sensed that he was saying to himself: 'Let these damn Yankees go home if they want to, they're just making a good thing out of us.' But what he did say, nostalgically, was: 'There was a time when Texas was as English as Australia . . . .'

(Joe is J.R. Ackerley. Warren is Warren Roberts, in charge of the HRC)

---

* Humanities Research Center.

Diary entry. Friday 5 February 1971.

Yesterday afternoon, getting more and more frustrated by the postal strike in England, I decided to ring London by telephone. I was amazed. I put the call through at 5.10 p.m. Austin time – ten minutes past midnight London time. I got through to Alexis, incredibly, in two minutes. I must have roused him in bed. He said at once: 'How exciting!' He assured me at once that everything was all right; that Rudy had had a miraculous cure for his rheumatism and was now gambolling around like a puppy; and promised to pass on my messages to Ros. and B. I said: 'I'm happily installed in Austin, it's a warm afternoon with temperature at nearly 70°F. He said: 'How marvellous!'

(Ros. and B. were my sisters Rosamond and Beatrix.)

Diary entry: Thursday 11 February.

I have been in much anxiety about the earthquake in California; and after trying all yesterday evening without avail, I managed to get hold of Christopher on the telephone. 'Are you and Don all right?' He replied: 'Yes, we're all right, but it was absolutely sensational. The tremors went on for a full minute, which is a long time for an earthquake. The whole house rocked and shook; of course it was not like being bombed, but we heard what we thought were violent explosions but it turned out to be the noise of pots and pans crashing to the ground in the kitchen. And then the tremors repeated themselves, but less violently, at intervals.' I said: 'You must have been terrified out of your wits.' He said, 'No, really we were paralysed with shock. The whole place of course is now full of refugees, living in schoolrooms and tents, with police cars going by just to see there's no looting . . . . You remember where we took the wrong turning on our way to Santa Barbara? Well, the epicentre was just there.'

Austin, Texas, 8 March 1971 (letter from J.L. to C.I.).

I did appreciate your hospitality on my brief visit to Los Angeles, and the special effort you made introducing me at UCLA*. I hereby vow to *prevent* anyone asking you to introduce me on any future occasion. I was deeply touched by what you said, and I won't have you exploited any more.

Also, how extremely pleasant it was to have a good talk with you and Don. I was thrilled to be able to see bits of *Kathleen and Frank* – my appetite was terribly whetted. And I have ordered the Columbia booklet; but wait most eagerly for the Twayne book.

I had one of those ghastly journeys back. They turned us off the plane (due to start at 4.50 p.m.) as there was a tiny wire that wasn't functioning. We didn't take off till 6.30 p.m., so I arrived in Austin at midnight – to find the patient Morris still waiting. They fed us on beastly sandwiches of synthetic turkey.

Morris, who is still a bit under the weather with his cold, sends love, as I do to you and Don.

* University of California, Los Angeles.

Diary entry: 10 March.

Last Thursday-Friday was my visit to Los Angeles, the lecture on V.W.* at UCLA, and the subsequent taking part in the seminar on Henry Green, with the teacher Carey Wall as my hostess and introducer. The lecture turned out, I thought, a great success, with a full hall (about 140 people) and interesting questions afterwards. Christopher, bless his heart, allowed himself to be sacrificed once more as introducer to me, and did me proud – too proud. The seminar was more like a bean-feast, the students arriving like children with the food, organizing everything (C.W. providing the drink), and washing up everything, giggling and shouting and carrying on and thoroughly enjoying themselves. I talked about Henry in general, and then they beseiged me with questions. A good time, I think, was had by all. I was particularly interested and pleased to meet a young graduate student, a pretty and very intelligent dark, petite girl, who was doing a study of the feminine sensibility in the modern English novel, with a long chapter on Rosamond's work. She seemed extremely perceptive and sensible, much admiring R.

I had the lunch period on Thursday with C. and Don, and then the evening after the seminar, and finally the morning on Friday. I thought C. in better form than last autumn, happier in himself, his blue eyes sparkling and darting, those spell-binding smiles perhaps a little less deliberate. I think he was very much relaxed by the enthusiasm with which his new book about his parents had been received by his publishers on

* Virginia Woolf.

both sides of the Atlantic . . .. We talked a lot about the earthquake, C. admitting that the after-shocks (all day long) were what began to get him down, and the paralyzing experience of the way the house groaned, clenched itself, and seemed to want to tear itself apart while the main shock was going on . . . . He showed me parts of the new book, which indicated that he was at last going to make no bones about his queerness. I thought it read excellently, and my appetite was much whetted. At the same time I was a bit worried that he had decided on the convention of speaking of himself as 'Christopher' all through, as if he found himself unable to speak without a mask. He defended himself by saying that if he had talked of his mother as 'my mother' irrelevant emotions would have been aroused; also that his childhood was so far away that it seemed like the childhood of a quite different person. At the same time, I couldn't help feeling that the reader might find a slight element of 'baby-talk' in it.

I was, I admit, surprised at his revelations about Wystan, that he had never told me of before: that they had had an affair that even went on, on an occasional basis, right up to the time when they reached the USA in 1939 . . . . C. and Don retired to his study, and I heard C. dictating (the Frankenstein treatment*), and Don typing.

(I think the 'new book' referred to here must have been *Christopher and His Kind*.)

---

* 'Frankenstein: the true story', an adaptation of Mary Shelley's book commissioned by Universal Studios.

Diary entry: San Diego, 5 November.

Douglas* has been gone one week now. I miss him very
much, not merely for meals prepared and flat looked after, his
welcoming me after late classes, but just for his presence.

We visited C. and Don at Santa Monica on 23 October.
C. his usual sweet self, very pleased with the excellent review I
had brought him of *Kathleen and Frank* (for the *Financial Times*,
by old Snow§ – who couldn't resist a side-swipe at
Bloomsbury). He presented me with a touchingly inscribed copy
of *K. & F.* We talked a great deal of the reviews of *Maurice*,
some of which have been very damp and stupid. I am growing
fond of the house in Adelaide Drive, and when we left on
Sunday felt a pang of regret, as if I had lived there myself a
long time – or might never see it again.

* Douglas Steere(?).
§ C.P. Snow.

San Diego, 25 November (letter from J.L. to C.I.).

I did so enjoy seeing you on Monday, and having that long walk over the mountain ridges in the afternoon.

The evening was curious, as these occasions generally are, but I think the elderly ladies and gents in business suits were entertained to be reminded of something they had long forgotten – the *Alice* books. Anyway, it was preceded by a first-class dinner party in the home of the Chairman of the LA English-Speaking Union, in as beautiful a home as I have seen in this part of the world (not excepting George Cukor's* house). A rich man, with enough to employ a truly first-class chef. Must be a member of the Mafia.

I enclose two more poems, as I threatened. When you have a moment, do let me know how they strike you.

* The American film director.

Diary entry: Friday 26 November – aftermath of Thanksgiving.

I suddenly realized that there were now only three weeks left before my return to London for Christmas. Almost incredible.

Last Monday I spent the whole day (and night) in Los Angeles, giving two lectures, both on Lewis Carroll and Nonsense. In the morning at the College of the Immaculate Heart, which turned out to be ex-Catholic, no nuns, and now an independent 'experimental' college of about 500 boys and girls; situated on a beautiful, steep slope in Hollywood, with lushly flowering shrubs all through the grounds. A small, informal group, very friendly; my host, Fallon Edwards, seemed very happy with the talk.

Afterwards I was called for by Christopher, and he drove me up to the Observatory in Griffith Park, where we went for a long walk over the mountain ridges, and talked endlessly of cabbages and kings, and what the days of yore were like, and what the future will bring. It reminded me of the long walk we took together in the Isle of Wight, over thirty years ago. This time, too, he talked of what he planned to write: it seems that he is engaged in the long work of revising and expanding the diaries he had kept since arriving in the US all that time ago, particularly filling in details of sexual encounters – which he said returned to his memory extremely vividly as soon as he found the notes in his diary. His earlier diary, he confessed, had been an inestimable mine for all the books he had written, scarcely anything usable was left (though I do remember passages I was shown that were utterly fascinating and never used). Now for a new series of books based on these later diaries.

Then he took me along to P.M.'s where we had drinks, and then I rested; and after that he took me along to the house of the Chairman of the ESU* – one of the most beautiful houses I have seen out here, as beautiful, in a different way, as George Cukor's. A large gathering for dinner, which was one of the very best I have eaten on this side of the ocean, cooked as well as any Parisian chef could achieve. Derek Jewell, publishing director of *The Times*, was among the guests. He said he remembered me talking – so long ago – to the Oxford Poetry Society in the first year of the war; Francis King,§ even Sidney Keyes#, I believe, were present. Then I was driven to the Ambassador Hotel, in the ballroom of which I gave my talk to about 250 assembled members of the ESU (the largest outside New York). Business executives mainly, I think, and white or blue-haired elderly ladies, with a sprinkling of younger people. Daunted rather by the ranks of wan faces; but soon Alice did the trick for me, and they came up with delight afterwards . . . . P.M. says I ought to do it much more often; well, I will – if they'll make it more worth my while.

* English Speaking Union.
§ The novelist and critic.
# The poet, killed in the Second World War.

Diary entry: Friday 21 July 1972.

Yesterday I went with David Carver* to a Buck. House garden party. Much as ever, but the flower borders even better, I thought, than last year, a feast of colour, scent and shape. Couldn't help admiring the performance the Queen puts on, the immense skill she shows. She goes through the pressing phalanx, she runs the gauntlet of the enormous crowds watching her, and has the selected groups presented to her: with the greatest ease and charm and dignity, has a word for every one of them, and behaves as if she were immensely interested and genuinely amused by the things they say to her! The timing is perfect.

Today, after an early lunch, to the first afternoon performance of *Cabaret* with Cousin Philip. The film has many faults: the cutting is bad, there is too much of the Master of Ceremonies, grotesquely amusing figure though Joel Grey makes him; and Liza Minnelli, in spite of an electrifying performance (it is really turned into a vehicle for her) is about as far from the original Sally Bowles as one can imagine – talk of not being able to get a part, even in the back row – she would have gone to the top right away! But the film is far nearer to the feeling of the original than the musical was, and Michael York gives a superb performance as the young Christopher: I was amazed at the likeness he managed to create by get-up and make-up, though the lips are too full and sensual to be exactly right. Very dishy indeed, one can't help falling for him. I thought it a pity that the crazy American, Clive, had been turned into a young German Baron, but the invention that he seduced both Sally and C. is really rather effective.
(Cousin Philip is Philip Mansel, first cousin twice removed, whom I had first come to know when he was at Eton.)

* Secretary to International P.E.N.

Diary entry: Saturday 10 January 1973.

Christopher rang this morning, to deliver his verdict on the parts (in draft) I have shown him of the Jack Marlowe book*. After a very short visit to London with Don (during the greater part of which he was cloistered with Don in David Hockney's flat working on the script of the Frankenstein film), he is off back to Santa Monica again, after briefly seeing friends in Switzerland and Rome (Salka Viertel and Gavin Lambert). I have seen very little of him – he and Don came for an hour one evening to No. 85, and I went for an hour to the flat – but he claimed when I grumbled a bit that I have seen more of him than most of his friends. He has, I think, been suffering from one of his (absurd, but partly consciously absurd) 'power' fits; and yet, in relation to what he is really worth, what more absurd than these TV films on Frankenstein and an Egyptian mummy. I am dismayed by them; though given great hope and enthusiasm by what I think really matters: his work on his diaries. I have never been convinced that he is a good script-writer for films or plays, in spite of all the great gifts he can bring to bear on them. I have never seen anything of his in that line that I thought good enough – from him.

He was definitely encouraging, in sober fashion, about Jack Marlowe, and urged me to press on as hard as I could. At the same time, he made several shrewd and valuable comments; most of which I agree with.

* *In the Purely Pagan Sense*, published by Blond and Briggs in 1976.

Cornwall Gardens, 18 July 1975 (letter from J.L. to C.I.).

The star of Christopher Isherwood is in the ascendant!

No sooner do I have a letter from William McBrien, editor of *Twentieth Century Literature*, to say that he's planning an Isherwood special number for next year and wants me to contribute, than another letter arrives from someone called Jonathan Fryer to say that he's writing a biography of you and wants to have a talk with me about it.*

Please let me know just as soon as you can whether Mr Fryer is a biographer who has your approval, and to what extent I am to be discreet/indiscreet.

As for Mr McBrien, it occurred to me that I might produce a piece for him on the genesis of *Goodbye to Berlin*, with extracts from all your letters referring to the preparation of the stories – quite a lot I think.

Would this be OK by you? And should I withhold your letters from Mr Fryer? If you don't mind him seeing some of them, perhaps you'd let me know those you *do* mind him seeing (or the other way round) – you have all the copies. I shan't be a bit surprised if you'd rather he didn't see them at all.

Do let me have a word as soon as you can, as they're practically knocking on my door. And of course let me know at the same time how near you are to finishing your book. Longing to know. Someone told me you had been working on a Fitzgerald script? Alexi and I send much love to you and Don. And Tommy,§ still looking after me excellently, adds a word of greeting too.

---

* Jonathan Fryer's *Isherwood, A Biography of Christopher Isherwood*, was published by the New English Library in 1977.
§ Thomas Laird, a friend of John Lehmann.

My Virginia Woolf* book comes out over here in
September, but the Harcourt Brace edition not till the New
Year. Wish I could see Don's paintings. Santa Barbara's off till
late 1976.

* *Virginia Woolf and her World* was published by Thames and Hudson.

Cornwall Gardens, 6 August 1975 (letter from J.L. to C.I.).

Very glad to get your letters, as they have already started to bombard me. I will use my discretion, and perhaps show very few letters indeed, apart from those in Texas (*New Writing* files) which can anyway be studied (but not of course quoted) by any bona fide student. Mr Brian Finney* is upon me next week – he rather took my breath away by asking me to spare 'one or two hours of my time' . . . . I think you'll find Jonathan Fryer rather sweet. A tall slim boy, camouflaging a sensitive and slightly feminine face with a large droopy moustache. Very shy, so much so that his voice becomes like the gnat's voice in *Alice* when he first talks to one. He has a sense of humour, and giggles a lot.

I will write that piece on the origins of *Goodbye to Berlin*, if Bill McBrien (who is extremely nice, and actually gave me lunch!) wants it after he reads my review of the Sally Bowles omnibus in the *Financial Times* – a sudden request by the literary editor after I'd spoken to McBrien. I loved your new introduction – masterly.

A reason for replying at once is that I have given your address to an extremely nice girl, Gillian Freeman, who is going to be over in Hollywood this month, perhaps with her husband, Ted, who's a ballet critic. Rather a good novelist (she wrote *The Leather Boys*), very intelligent and amusing, loves Los Angeles where she has done work. She wrote the script of the Virginia Woolf TV film on which I collaborated with her. I do hope you won't mind; but I think you and Don should enjoy meeting her. A great fan of yours. About your book. My own

---

* Author of *Christopher Isherwood, A Critical Biography*, published by Faber and Faber in 1979.

instinct is to say: publish the part up to 1939 separately, as soon as you have finished it. Not merely because the American part may, as you suggest, upset the balance, but because it will make it a very long and tremendously *expensive* book. Why shouldn't there be three volumes? It seems to me an excellent idea.

We are in the middle of a heat wave, incredible. Tea, lunch, breakfast on the lawn at the Cottage. Alexi, browner and browner every day, sends love, as I do, to both of you, and Tommy sends more greetings.

Cornwall Gardens, 6 September 1975 (letter from J.L. to C.I.)

Just a line, to say that your press-cutting agency may send you a copy of a review I wrote about 'The Berlin of Sally Bowles' in the *Financial Times*, in which you may be surprised to find mention of a character unknown to you – *and to me* – called 'Marge'! This extraordinary misprint/invention is due, I am told, to the Head Reader's confusion in the *FT*'s office as the page went to press. They send their profound apologies, and no doubt a little note will appear under my next review. Maddening. I hope it will make you laugh rather than cry; but I boiled. With a name like that, I don't think she can have been a friend of Sally's, do you? . . .

Adelaide Drive, 31 July 1977 (letter from C.I. to J.L.).

You ask about the progress of the book – but I think maybe you don't know that I'm working on a memoir of my life in the nineteen forties, in California. (*That* is very thoroughly documented in my diaries.) However I decided to do my memories of life with Swami Prabhavananda first – which runs from 1939 to 1976, when he died . . .

Adelaide Drive, 13 March 1978 (letter from C.I. to J.L.).

The Lear book*, which I've meanwhile received, is absolutely beautiful, *and* beautiful to look at. I suppose he had his fun, one way and another, but it is nevertheless a poignant story, don't you think, despite all his genius and successful career? You tell it excellently. I greatly look forward to *Thrown to the Woolfs*§! Yes, of course, quote anything you want from my letters – copies are unnecessary.

My book about the Swami is at least in a rough draft, plus 50 pages rewritten, but it's still hard work, and will offend many. There is also a project to publish a book of Don's drawings, with a commentary on the sitters by both of us. This seems nearly definite . . . .

* *Edward Lear and his World*, published in 1977 by Thames and Hudson.
§ *Thrown to the Woolfs* was published by Weidenfeld & Nicolson in 1978.

Cornwall Gardens, 21 November 1983 (letter from J.L. to C.I.).

I've just been sent some clippings about the Auden celebrations in New York, which seem to have become a rather memorable occasion. And a clipping (from the *NY Times*) about an interview with you personally, which has fascinated me. I congratulate you on receiving the Award from the Modern Languages Association: I wish you could receive something similar over here.

I long to hear that you have completed the book you are at work on at present. Alexis is as eager as I am to read it.

My book on *Three Literary Friendships* has come out over here*, but won't be out on your side of the ocean until the New Year. I will have Billy Abrahams§ send you an early copy. I long to know what you think of it. I am now at work – rather slowly – on my final volume of Memoirs – haven't got a title for it yet.

I had rather a nasty fall a few weeks ago. Very stupid, and mostly due to the uneven pavements just round here. I am much better now, but it was a bit of a shock.

When are you coming over? We all miss you very much, and are pining to see you. Do write me a line or two about your work and your plans. A happy Christmas to you and Don – with much love.

---

* Published by Quartet.
§ An editor at the American publishers Holt Reinhart, also a biographer.

INDEX

Abrahams, Billy, 142
Ackerley, J.R. (Joe), 123, 124*n*
Address Not Known (projected Auden/
   Isherwood book), 49
'Adventures of the Black Girl in her
   Search for God' (Shaw), 117
'Afterwards' (Isherwood), 98-100
'Alfred', 65
All the Conspirators (Isherwood), 2, 8,
   9, 46, 108
'Ambrose' (part of *Down There on a
   Visit*) (Isherwood), 64, 96, 97
Ample Proposition, The (Lehmann), 107
Amsterdam, 20, 24-5, 26
Ascent of F.6, The (Auden/Isherwood),
   22, 32, 51
Atlanta, 113
Auden, Wystan H., 19, 61, 116,
   119; early friendship with
   Isherwood, 1, 46; in Berlin, 8,
   12, 15; description of Isherwood,
   10; playwriting with Isherwood,
   22, 32, 47, 51; and *New Writing*,
   25, 26; and Spanish Civil War,
   35, 36, 40; in China with
   Isherwood, 38, 40-43, 47; in New
   York, 43-4, 74, 93, 142; publish-
   ing plot, 48-9; emigration to
   America, 48, 50; drift from
   Isherwood over Yoga, 53-4;
   vilified as 'deserter', 54-5, 72;
   continuing friendship with
   Isherwood, 108; early affair with
   Isherwood, 129
Austin (Texas), 113, 124-5, 127

Bachardy, Don, 2, 80; permanent
   alliance with Isherwood, 84-5,
   86-7, 93, 95, 108, 120, 121, 122,
   127, 128, 129, 130, 137, 138,
   141; artistic career, 86, 95, 102,
   106, 117; as portraitist, 86, 106,
   119, 141; work on film scripts
   with Isherwood, 117, 129, 135
Bachardy, Ted, 84
Baxter, Walter, 83
Beesley, Alec, 51, 78

Bell, Julian, 7
Berkeley College, San Francisco,
   113, 120
Berlin, 8, 9, 12-15, 47, 81, 83
'Berlin of Sally Bowles, The'
   (Isherwood), 140
Bhagavad-Gita, 63-4, 68
Blanc-Roos, Réné, 66
Bodley Head, The, 25, 39*n*
Bowen, Elizabeth, 39
Bower, Tony, 35, 68
Bowles, Paul, 86, 87
Bradbury, Ray, 82
Bradshaw, John, 107
Brussels, 23, 26, 29, 31, 35, 36,
   37-8, 47
Buenos Aires, 76
Byron, Lord, 115
Bubi, 12, 44, 76
Burford, Roger, 2

Cabaret (musical and film), 109,
   114, 117, 134
Calcutta, 104
Cambridge, 1, 2, 47
Canary Islands, 20-22
Canton, 41
Cape, Jonathan, Limited, 2, 8
Capote, Truman, 82
Carver, David, 134
Caskey, Bill, alliance with, 67, 74,
   76, 77, 78, 79, 81
Chambers, Robert, 4
Chamson, André, 28
Chaplin, Charlie, 59, 67
Chaplin, Oona, 67
Cheltenham, 72
Chesterton, G.K., 93
Chinese-Japanese war, 38, 40-43
'Christ the Hunter' (Lehmann), 104
'Christopher Garland' (Isherwood), 2
Christopher and His Kind (Isherwood),
   12, 15, 32, 43, 129; quoted, 11,
   25, 29, 47
*Christopher Isherwood, A Critical
   Biography* (Finney), 138*n*
City and the Pillar, The (Vidal), 77

Clark-Kerr, Sir Archibald, 42, 43
Coal-Face (film), 26
Cockburn, Claud, 16
Cocteau, Jean, 44, 79, 107
Collins, Wilkie, 67
'Coming to London' (Isherwood),
    69-71, 73
Condor and the Cows, The (Isherwood),
    67, 78
Connolly, Cyril, 35, 55, 66
Connolly, Jean, 35, 66
Conrad, Joseph, 93
Copenhagen, 22, 23
Cornelius, Henry, 92
Crowley, Aleister, 87
Cukor, George, 131, 133
Curtis Brown, 8

Davis, George, 43
'Day at La Verne, A' (Isherwood),
    57-8, 65
Daylight, 41
Diane de Poitiers (film script), 80, 92
Dog Beneath the Skin, The (Auden/
    Isherwood), 15, 22, 32, 117
Donat, Robert, 59
Doone, Rupert, 22
Dostoevsky, Feodor, 77
Down There on a Visit (Isherwood),
    48, 66, 94; origin and episodes
    of, 64, 81, 94, 95-7; auto-
    biographical element, 95-6;
    Lehmann's opinion of, 96-7, 103;
    disappointing reviews, 101
Doyle, Sir Arthur Conan, 93
Duras, Marguerite, 105

Edward Lear and his World (Lehmann),
    141
Edwards, Fallon, 132
Eliot, T.S., 49
Elizabeth II, Queen, 134
Emory College, Atlanta, 113
Empson, William, 42
Encounter, 53n, 123
English-Speaking Union, 131, 133
'Englishman, An', original title of
    A Single Man, 102

Estoril, 31, 34
Evening Standard, 78
Evil Was Abroad (Lehmann), 33-4, 72
Exhumations (Isherwood), 86, 105-6
Eyre and Spottiswoode, 107n

Faber and Faber, 40, 49
Faust (Goethe), 13
Financial Times, 130, 138, 140
Finney, Brian, 138
Fodor, Ladislas, 77
Forster, E.M., 52, 93, 101, 119, 123-4;
    homosexual short stories, 98,
    100, 121
Fouts, Denny, 65-6, 77, 96
Frankenstein: the true story (film), 129, 135
Freeman, Gillian, 138
Freshwater Bay (I.o.W.), 46
Fronny, The - see *Dog Beneath the Skin*
Fry, Basil, 95
Fryer, Jonathan, 136, 138
Furbank, P.N., 121, 123

Gambler, The (Dostoevsky), 77
Garbo, Greta, 52, 59, 67
Gaumont British, 18, 64
George VI, King, 82
Gielgud, John, 93, 105
Giese, Karl, 15
Goodbye to Berlin (Isherwood), 33, 78,
    94, 97; genesis of, 29, 136, 138,
    140; failure in America, 51, 109;
    English success, 57.
    See also *I am a Camera*
Graves, Robert, 93
Great English Short Stories (comp.
    Isherwood), 93
Great Sinner, The (film), 77
Green, Henry, 83, 128
Greene, Graham, 21
Grey, Joel, 134
Group Theatre, 15, 22, 36, 44
Gwynn, Michael, 90

Hamilton, Gerald, 14, 23, 35, 55;
    original of Mr Norris, 21
Hammersley, Violet, 7, 45
Hankow, 42

Harcourt Brace, 137
Harper's Bazaar, 41
Harris, Julie, 78
Hartford (Connecticut), 78
Haverford (Philadelphia), 66
'Head of a Leader, The' (Isherwood), 53*n*
Heard, Gerald, 51, 52, 58, 66; and Yoga, 53, 57, 62-3
Heinz – *see* Neddermayer, Heinz
Hilton, James, 58, 59
Hindenberg, Paul von, 13
Hitler, Adolf, 13, 48
Hockney, David, 135
Hogarth Press, 41; Lehmann as trainee manager, 7-8, 12; as Isherwood's publisher, 29, 33, 49, 108; Lehmann as partner in, 38-9, 46, 49
Hollywood, 51-68, 92, 105, 132, 138
Holt, Rinehart and Winston, 143*n*
Hong Kong, 41, 42, 43
Horizon, 55, 66
Hour Before Dawn, The (Maugham), 67
Huston, John, 105
Huxley, Aldous, 64; in Hollywood, 51, 52, 53, 58, 67; death, 104
Huxley, Julian, 104

I, Claudius (film), 118
I am my Brother (Lehmann), 94
I am a Camera (Van Druten): dramatization from *Goodbye to Berlin* and *Sally Bowles*, 51, 78-9; brilliant success, 79, 80, 89-90; film and musical versions, 79, 92; see also *Cabaret*
In Cold Blood (Capote), 82
In the Purely Pagan Sense (Lehmann), 135
Isherwood, Christopher: his work brought to Lehmann's notice, 8-9, 108; first meeting with Lehmann, 10-12; crucial journey to Berlin, 12-14; dream of 'German Boy', 12, 44, 76; homosexual affairs, 12, 15-17, 19-22, 43-4, 47, 52, 65-6, 67, 79, 81, 84-5, 129; escape from Berlin after Nazi control, 14-15,

19-22; worry over danger of war, 16, 23, 48, 52; introduction to film work, 18-19; work on *Mr Norris Changes Trains*, 21, 22; playwriting collaboration with Auden, 22, 32, 38, 47, 51; European wanderings, 23-4, 31-6; and *New Writing*, 24-30, 33, 36, 52; genesis of *Sally Bowles* and other Berlin stories, 27, 28-9, 38, 39; advice on Lehmann's work, 33-4, 109, 135; journey to China, 38, 40-43, 47; fantastic story-telling, 45, 47; unwritten novel, 46, 64; emigration to America, 47, 48, 50-51; publishing plot, 49; erotic tangle, 49, 57; pacifism, 51, 54, 61, 62, 109; in Hollywood, 51 *et seq.*; conversion to Yoga, 53-4, 59, 62, 66; obsession with sainthood, 54, 80; vilified as 'deserter', 54-5; intention not to return to England, 55; and Vedanta, 55-8, 59, 62-4, 65, 84, 109; writing block, 58, 62, 64, 66, 106; writing of film scripts, 58-60, 67, 77, 78, 80, 92, 105, 117, 118, 129, 135; feeling of alienation from friends in England, 61-2, 68; with Quakers, 66; becomes American subject, 67, 70; post-war visits to England, 69-74, 81-2, 83-5, 106; happiness in resumed friendships, 70, 72, 83, 84, 108; absorption in film-world, 72; in South America, 76, 77; finances, 78-9, 80, 114; 'worst novel', 80; trip to Mexico, 80; return to Berlin, 82-3; beginning of permanent alliance with Don Bachardy, 84-5, 86-7; permanent home in Santa Monica, 87; unpublishable homosexual short story, 98-100; professorship, 102, 106; bereavements, 104; book about parents, 106-7, 114, 117, 119, 121, 127, 128, 130; 'religious novel', 107; firm friendship with

Isherwood - contd.:
  Lehmann, 108-9; Australasian
  trip, 117, 118; and California
  earthquake, 126, 129; revelation
  of homosexuality, 129; early affair
  with Auden, 129; revision of
  diaries, 132, 135; biographies of,
  136, 138
Isherwood, Lt-Colonel Francis B.
  (father), 1, 106, 114
Isherwood, Kathleen (mother), 16,
  19, 52, 57, 68, 114, 129; artistic
  tastes, 1; financial aid to
  Isherwood, 2, 35; wartime in
  Wales, 48; post-war reunion with
  Isherwood, 72; recovery from
  stroke, 93; death, 104; fixation
  with husband as hero-figure, 106
Isherwood, Richard (brother), 48, 72
Isherwood, A Biography of Christopher
  Isherwood (Fryer), 136n

Jacob's Hands (film script), 67
Jagger, Mick, 118
Jewell, Derek, 133
Journey to the Border (Upward), 39
Journey to a War (Auden/Isherwood),
  43, 47

Kallman, Chester, 50, 76
Kathleen and Frank (Isherwood), 106,
  107, 114, 127, 128, 130
Kennedy, Margaret, 19
Keyes, Sidney, 133
King, Francis, 133
Kipling, Rudyard, 93
Kiskadden, Margaret, 63
Krishnamurti, 59

La Verne College, Southern
  California, 57-8, 66
Laird, Tommy, 136, 139
Lambert, Gavin, 135
Lamkin, Speed, 82, 89
Lanchester, Elsa, 87, 121
'Landauers, The' (Isherwood), 29, 39
Lane, Allen, 25
Lane, Homer, 12

Laughton, Charles, 87, 104
Lawrence, D.H., 93
Lawrence & Wishart, 39
Lear, Edward, 141
Left Review, 24
Lehmann, Alice Marie, 8, 45, 46
Lehmann, Beatrice (Peggy), 17, 19,
  46, 47, 52, 89, 104, 121, 125;
  friendship with Isherwood, 13;
  stage performances, 41, 43, 44, 73
Lehmann, John: as trainee manager in
  Hogarth Press, 7-8, 12; introduced
  to Isherwood's work, 8-9, 108; first
  meeting, 10-12; in Vienna, 12,
  15, 20, 28, 38; visit to Isherwood
  in Berlin, 13-14; founding of New
  Writing, 24-9; and genesis of
  Goodbye to Berlin, 28-30; his own
  writings, 33-4, 90, 91, 94, 107,
  135, 137, 141, 142; as partner in
  Hogarth Press, 38-9, 41, 46, 49;
  extricates Isherwood from erotic
  tangle, 49, 57; and Isherwood's
  post-war visits to England, 70, 72,
  74, 83-4; founds own firm, 74;
  founds London Magazine, 79, 91,
  94; 'opening of hearts' with
  Isherwood, 83; life in Sussex
  cottage, 84, 90, 103, 139; lecturing
  and visiting professorships at
  American universities, 87, 106,
  113, 120, 123-4, 128, 132; firm
  friendship with Isherwood, 108-9;
  visits Isherwood in California,
  119, 121-2, 127-31
Lehmann, John, Limited, 74, 83
Lehmann, Rosamond, 8, 41, 43,
  125, 128
Lehmann, Rudolph Chambers, 117
Lions and Shadows (Isherwood), 12,
  33, 94; origin and writing of, 9,
  32, 36, 39
London Magazine, 69, 79, 89, 91, 94,
  107, 113
London Mercury, 24
Longmans, 94
Look Down in Mercy (Baxter), 83

Lopokova, Lydia, 47
Lord Byron (Thomson), 115
Los Angeles, 121, 122, 127, 128-9, 132-3, 138
'Lost, The' (Isherwood) (later *Mr Norris Changes Trains*, q.v.), 18, 22, 25, 29, 38, 41
Loved One, The (film), 105
Lucas, Major Sir Jocelyn, 54
Luxembourg, 36-7

McBrien, William, 136, 138
McCullers, Carson, 105
MacNeice, Louis, 54
Mailer, Norman, 82
Mangeot, Olive, 73
Mann, Heinrich, 59
Mann, Thomas, 59
Mansel, Philip, 134
Mansfield, Katherine, 93
Martin, Kenneth, 116
Maugham, Somerset, 67, 93
Maurice (Forster), 119, 121, 130
Mayne, Ethel, 93
Meeting by the River, A (Isherwood), 104; attempt at religious novel, 107-8; rewritten as play and film script, 108, 117, 119*n*
Memorial, The (Isherwood), 11, 18, 36, 96; his first novel published by Hogarth Press, 8, 9, 108
Menuhin, Yehudi, 104
Methuen and Co., 32, 76, 80, 103*n*, 105
Metro-Goldwyn-Mayer, 58, 59-60, 77, 78, 80
Minelli, Liza, 79, 134
'Mr Lancaster' (Isherwood) (part of *Down There on a Visit*), 94, 95-6, 97
Mr Norris Changes Trains (Isherwood), 21, 22, 36, 108
Modern Languages Association, 143
Moore, George, 93
Mortal Storm, The (film), 59
Mourning Becomes Electra (O'Neill), 41, 43
Munich Agreement (1938), 47, 48, 54

'My Enemy' (Chamson), 28
My Guru and his Disciple (Isherwood), 63, 66, 85, 141
Mystery of Edwin Drood, The (Dickens), 103

Neddermayer, Heinz, 27, 52, 54, 64, 95; liaison with Isherwood, 15-17; attempt to get into England, 19-20; European wanderings, 20-22, 23-4, 31, 32, 35, 46; attempts to change nationality, 23, 34-5, 37; trouble with French police, 36; arrest for draft-evasion and moral offences, 37-8; marriage, 47, 83; Berlin reunion with Isherwood, 83
New Country, 24
New English Library, 136*n*
New Signatures, 24
New Soundings, 81-2
New World Writing, 90
New Writing, 38-9, 41, 46, 108, 113, 138; founding of, 24-9; Isherwood contributions, 33, 36, 52
New York, 43-4, 50-51, 74-5
New York Times, 97
No More Music (R. Lehmann), 41, 43
'North-West Passage' (Isherwood), 36, 38; see also *Lions and Shadows*
'Nowaks, The' (Isherwood), 27, 36, 56, 108

O'Neill, Eugene, 43
Observer, 82, 83
Ocampo, Vittoria, 76
On the Frontier (Auden/Isherwood), 22, 38, 47
'Other Boat, The' (Forster), 121
Otto, 15
Oxford, 39
Oxford Poetry Society, 133

Paris, 35, 76
Passing of the Third Floor Back, The (film), 19
'Paul is Alone' (Isherwood), 32, 46, 64
Penguin New Writing, 56, 57, 65, 74, 76

Plomer, William, 28, 93, 115
Prabhavananda, Swami, 55, 63, 64, 66, 104; Isherwood's book on, 141
Prater Violet (Isherwood), 19, 64, 66, 79, 97, 109
Pritchett, V.S., 93
Pro Helvetia Foundation, 103
'Problems of the Religious Novel' (Isherwood), 54, 80
Proust, Marcel, 21
Put Out More Flags (Waugh), 55

Quartet Books, 143*n*
Quennell, Peter, 107

Rage in Heaven (film), 59
'Railway Accident, The' (Upward), 2, 28, 119
Ramakrishna, 92, 102
Ramakrishna and his Disciples (Isherwood), 102, 104, 105
Random House, 40, 76, 80, 90, 92
Rassine, Alexis, 84, 89, 90, 103, 125, 136, 139, 142
Reflections in a Golden Eye (film), 105
Reinhardt, Gottfried, 59
Repton, 1, 2, 46*n*
Richardson, Tony, 105, 118
Roberts, Michael, 24*n*
Roberts, Warren, 124
Ross, Jean, 73; original of Sally Bowles, 18, 27, 29
Russell, Bertrand, 59
Rylands, George, 7

Sacco, Nicola, 77
Sailor from Gibraltar, The (film), 105
St Nicholas (Greek island), 15-16
Sally Bowles (Isherwood), 41, 42; genesis of, 27; publication, 28-9; incorporated in *Goodbye to Berlin*, 29; dramatic and film versions, 78-9, 108; *see also Cabaret; I am a Camera*
San Diego (California), 113, 119, 130-1
San Francisco, 113

Santa Barbara, 102, 106, 122
Santa Monica (California), Isherwood's last home in, 70, 77, 87, 95, 119, 120, 121, 130, 135
Sassoon, Sir Victor, 42
Schorer, Mark, 120
'Seascape with Figures'-see *All the Conspirators*
'September 1st 1939' (Auden), 55
Shaw, Bernard, 117*n*
Shelley, Mary, 129*n*
Single Man, A (Isherwood), 77, 97, 102, 103
Sintra, 27-8, 31-2, 34
Sloss, D.J., 41
Smith, Dodie, 51, 78
Snow, C.P., 130
Southern, Terry, 105
Spanish Civil War, 34, 35, 40
Spender, Erica, 22
Spender, Inez, 36
Spender, Michael, 22
Spender, Stephen, 8-9, 27, 31, 61, 93
Steere, Douglas, 130
Steiner, Rudolf, 32
Stern, James, 35, 74
Stern, Tania, 35
Stravinsky, Igor, 81
Styron, William, 82
Sur, 76

Tangier, 86
Tenerife, 20-22
Thames and Hudson, 137*n*, 141*n*
Thomas, Dylan, 93
Thomson, Virgil, 115
Three Literary Friendships (Lehmann), 142
Thrown to the Woolfs (Lehmann), 141
Thurau, Fräulein, 83
Toller, Ernst, 53
Totland Bay (I.o.W.), 45, 46
Trier, 37
Turville-Petre, Francis, 14-16
Tutin, Dorothy, 79, 90
Twentieth Century Literature, 136

Universal Studios, 129*n*

University of California: Los Angeles, 128-9; San Diego, 113; Santa Barbara, 102, 106
University of Texas, Austin, 113, 124
Upward, Edward, 26, 80, 94; friendship with Isherwood, 1-2, 8, 46; and Mortmere fantasy world, 2, 119; his critical approval important to Isherwood, 2, 27, 95; his own work, 28, 39, 119

Van Druten, John, 51, 78, 89
Van der Lubbe, Marinus, 13
Vancouver, 43
Vanzetti, Bartolomeo, 77
Vaughan, Keith, 74
Vedanta, 55, 59, 63, 65, 84, 109
Vedanta and the West, 54, 80
'Vernon': liaison with Isherwood, 43-4, 47, 49, 65; as representative 'American Boy', 44; in Hollywood, 50, 51, 52; return to New York, 65, end of relationship, 67
Vidal, Gore, 76
Vienna, 12, 15, 20, 28, 38
Viertel, Berthold, 58; as film and stage director, 18-19, 41, 52; as Bergmann in Prater Violet, 19, 64
Viertel, Salka, 19, 52, 59, 67, 135
Virginia Woolf and her World (Lehmann), 137
'Visit to Anselm Oakes' (Isherwood), 86
Vivekananda, Swami, 104
Voix Humaine, La (Cocteau), 44

Wall, Carey, 128
Warner Brothers, 67
Watson, Peter, 66, 77

Waugh, Evelyn, 55, 105
Week, The, 16
Weidenfeld and Nicolson, 141n
Wells, H.G., 93
Weybright, Victor, 90
Where is Francis? - see Dog Beneath the Skin
Whispering Gallery, The (Lehmann), 90n
White, Alan, 80, 91
Wight, Isle of, 45-7, 132
Williams, Clifford, 119n
Williams, Tennessee, 65
Willingham, Calder, 82
Wintle, Hector, 46
Woman in White, The (Collins), 67
Wood, Christopher, 52
Woolf, Leonard, 121; and Hogarth Press, 7, 8, 9, 29, 32-3, 39
Woolf, Virginia: and Hogarth Press, 7, 8, 9, 29; neglect of Isherwood, 33, 39; Lehmann's lecture, book and film script on, 128, 137, 138
World in the Evening, The (Isherwood), 103; slow writing of, 74, 79, 80; Lehmann's opinion of, 80, 89, 90; as Isherwood's 'worst novel', 80; handling of dialogue and queer theme, 80, 91-2
Wyberslegh Hall (Cheshire), 1, 72

Yale, John, 107
Yoga, 53-4, 58, 62
York, Michael, 134
'Younger, Jimmy', 31